1st EDITION

Perspectives on Diseases and Disorders

Leukemia

Adrienne Wilmoth Lerner
Book Editor

PERSPECTIVES
On Diseases & Disorders

GALE
CENGAGE Learning·

Detroit • New York • San Francisco • New Haven, Conn • Waterville, Maine • London

Christine Nasso, *Publisher*
Elizabeth Des Chenes, *Managing Editor*

For more information, contact:
Greenhaven Press
27500 Drake Rd.
Farmington Hills, MI 48331-3535
Or you can visit our Internet site at gale.cengage.com

Articles in Greenhaven Press anthologies are often edited for length to meet page requirements. In addition, original titles of these works are changed to clearly present the main thesis and to explicitly indicate the author's opinion. Every effort is made to ensure that Greenhaven Press accurately reflects the original intent of the authors. Every effort has been made to trace the owners of copyrighted material.

Cover image copyright Sebastian Kaulitzki, 2008. Used under license of Shutterstock.com.

LIBRARY OF CONGRESS CATALOGING-IN-PUBLICATION DATA

Leukemia / Adrienne Wilmoth Lerner, book editor.
    p. cm. — (Perspectives on diseases and disorders)
  Includes bibliographical references and index.
  ISBN 978-0-7377-4247-3 (hardcover)
  1. Leukemia—Juvenile literature. I. Lerner, Adrienne Wilmoth.
  RC643.L42 2009
  616.99'419—dc22

                                                           2008052594

Printed in the United States of America
1 2 3 4 5 6 7 13 12 11 10 09

CONTENTS

local population. Possible pollution sources from local industries and a military base come under scrutiny as researchers investigate a cluster of childhood leukemia in Fallon, Nevada.

CHAPTER 2 Leukemia Issues and Controversies

genetic screening to ensure that a fetus is a matching donor. Others are concerned about the psychological well-being of "donor children," or whether they will be able to freely consent to medical procedures.

CHAPTER 3 Patients, Families, and Survivors Cope
with Leukemia

FOREWORD

"Medicine, to produce health, has to examine disease."
—Plutarch

Independent research on a health issue is often the first step to complement discussions with a physician. But locating accurate, well-organized, understandable medical information can be a challenge. A simple Internet search on terms such as "cancer" or "diabetes," for example, returns an intimidating number of results. Sifting through the results can be daunting, particularly when some of the information is inconsistent or even contradictory. The Greenhaven Press series Perspectives on Diseases and Disorders offers a solution to the often overwhelming nature of researching diseases and disorders.

From the clinical to the personal, titles in the Perspectives on Diseases and Disorders series provide student and other researchers with authoritative, accessible information in unique anthologies that include basic information about the disease or disorder, controversial aspects of diagnosis and treatment, and first-person accounts of those impacted by the disease. The result is a well-rounded combination of primary and secondary sources that, together, provide the reader with a better understanding of the disease or disorder.

Each volume in Perspectives on Diseases and Disorders explores a particular disease or disorder in detail. Material for each volume is carefully selected from a wide range of sources, including encyclopedias, journals, newspapers, nonfiction books, speeches, government documents, pamphlets, organization newsletters, and position papers. Articles in the first chapter provide an authoritative, up-to-date overview that covers symptoms, causes and effects, treatments, cures, and medical advances. The second chapter presents a substantial number of opposing viewpoints on controversial treatments and other current debates relating to the volume topic. The third chapter offers a variety of personal perspectives on the disease or disorder. Patients, doctors, caregivers, and loved ones represent just some of the voices found in this narrative chapter.

Each Perspectives on Diseases and Disorders volume also includes:

- An **annotated table of contents** that provides a brief summary of each article in the volume.
- An **introduction** specific to the volume topic.
- Full-color **charts and graphs** to illustrate key points, concepts, and theories.
- Full-color **photos** that show aspects of the disease or disorder and enhance textual material.
- **"Fast Facts"** that highlight pertinent additional statistics and surprising points.
- A **glossary** providing users with definitions of important terms.
- A **chronology** of important dates relating to the disease or disorder.
- An annotated list of **organizations to contact** for students and other readers seeking additional information.
- A **bibliography** of additional books and periodicals for further research.
- A detailed **subject index** that allows readers to quickly find the information they need.

Whether a student researching a disorder, a patient recently diagnosed with a disease, or an individual who simply wants to learn more about a particular disease or disorder, a reader who turns to Perspectives on Diseases and Disorders will find a wealth of information in each volume that offers not only basic information, but also vigorous debate from multiple perspectives.

INTRODUCTION

In 2000 a young neuroblastoma patient named Alex Scott started selling lemonade to raise money for childhood cancer research; the lemonade stands caught on across the United States. Alex lost her battle with childhood cancer in 2004, but her charitable foundation continues to thrive and has raised over $20 million.

The stories of courageous young cancer survivors and patients are compelling. As the leading form of pediatric cancer, leukemia is often a part of those stories. Characters in popular young adult books and TV shows cope with leukemia. Telethons profile leading research and treatment centers and feature the stories of children and doctors fighting leukemia. Families often know a child from

Telethons and fund-raising drives have raised both funds and public awareness of childhood leukemia.
(Photo by Alberto Tamargo/ Getty Images)

school or their community who is battling leukemia. Jars collecting donations for a child's transplant and treatment are common sights at grocery and convenience stores.

Because challenges to childhood resonate so strongly with people, childhood leukemia is one of the most well funded and studied of the serious pediatric diseases. The telethons, fund-raising drives, and lemonade stands have raised both funds and public awareness of the disease. As a result of charitable giving and medical research breakthroughs, the fight against childhood leukemia has enjoyed remarkable recent success. A generation ago, a diagnosis of childhood leukemia was a death sentence. Today, the five-year survival rate for early childhood ALL (acute lymphocytic, or lymphoblastic, leukemia) is almost 90 percent.

Leukemia can occur at any age. Often lost in the public focus on childhood leukemia is the plight of adult patients. Seniors over sixty years old remain the age group most affected by leukemia. Leukemias in adults have five-year survival rates far lower than pediatric leukemia. Few facilities for adults offer the level of family support given at pediatric centers.

The stories of adult leukemia patients and survivors may be less publicized, but they are no less compelling. Blogs written by patients capture the challenges of working, raising a family, and coping with illness. Some adults with leukemia face the disease for a second time after many years of being cancer-free following a childhood leukemia diagnosis. Those same Internet diaries often turn into a place of remembrance and mourning after a patient's final post.

Whether affecting children or adults, a leukemia story rarely involves only a patient and his or her doctors. A diagnosis of leukemia affects patients, doctors, friends, families, communities, and sometimes perfect strangers. Many leukemia narratives involve individuals who become part of a patient's treatment in a unique sense:

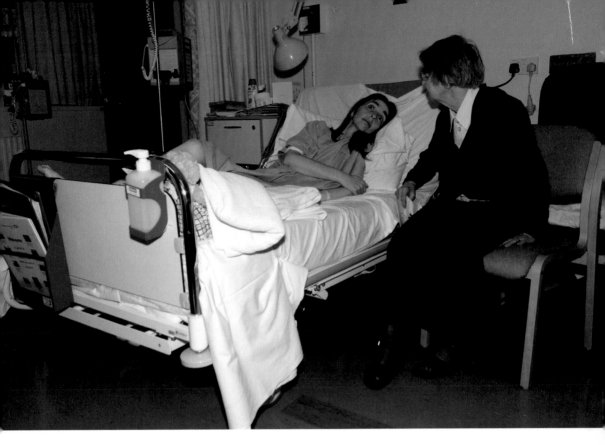

Friends, family, and community members get tested and rally to find a matching donor for an ailing person. Family members donate blood, plasma, and stem cells. Individuals participate in national marrow registries and are later called upon to provide bone marrow for strangers.

Children and adults, researchers and physicians, patients and caregivers, families and strangers: Their individual experiences may be different, yet they share a common desire for leukemia-free lives. But the struggle against leukemia remains far from won. In contrast to the success stories for those afflicted with ALL, survival rates for both pediatric and adult AML (acute myelogenous, or myeloid, leukemia) lag far behind those of ALL. Less is known about rarer forms of leukemia, such as hairy cell and mantle cell leukemias, than their more common counterparts. Researchers still search for a complete understanding of the development and progression of chronic leukemia. The search continues for less-toxic

In the battle against leukemia, the experiences of children and adults, researchers and physicians, and patients and caregivers may vary, but they all share a desire for leukemia-free lives. (© Tony Hobbs/Alamy)

chemotherapy drugs and less-invasive means of testing and transplantation.

Many leukemia experts feel they have reason for optimism, however. In spite of the difficulties with transplants and chemotherapy, these methods of treatment are fairly safe and often quite effective. Improved drugs help manage side effects and transplant rejection diseases. Stem cell and genetic research promise future breakthroughs. Patients are receiving better care for both the physical and emotional effects of leukemia; so too are their family members and caretakers. While a cure for leukemia may not be on the immediate horizon, medical advancements will continue to increase the likelihood of patient survival.

CHAPTER 1

Understanding Leukemia

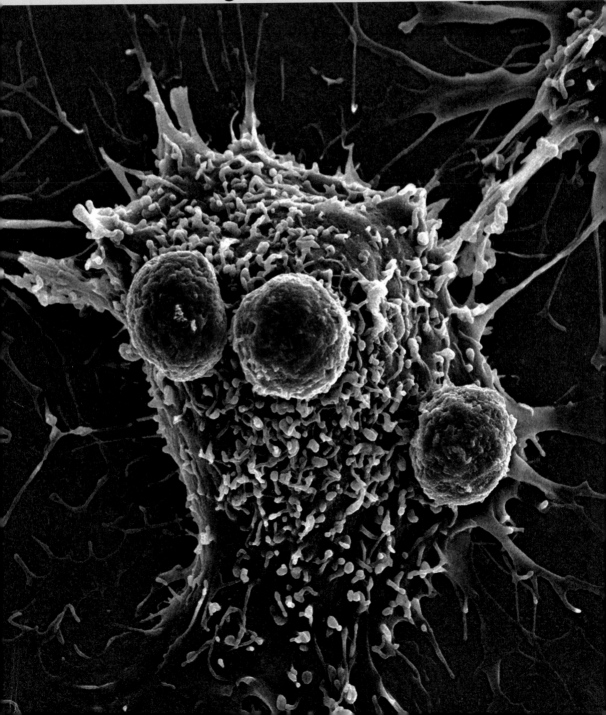

An Overview of Chronic Leukemias

Lata Cherath

In the following selection science writer Lata Cherath provides a general overview of the symptoms, diagnosis, progression, and treatment of chronic leukemias. Cherath discusses the differences between chronic lymphocytic leukemia (CLL) and chronic myeloid leukemia (CML), as well as the higher incidence of chronic leukemias in older individuals. Cherath was the science writing intern at the Cancer Research Institute in New York, New York, and is the editor of the *Gale Encyclopedia of Cancer*.

Chronic leukemia is a disease in which too many white blood cells are made in the bone marrow. Depending on the type of white blood cell that is involved, chronic leukemia can be classified as chronic lymphocytic leukemia or chronic myeloid leukemia.

Photo on previous page. An electron micrograph of T lymphocyte cells (red) attached to a cancer cell. **(Steve Gschmeissner/ Photo Researchers, Inc.)**

SOURCE: Lata Cherath, *Gale Encyclopedia of Medicine*. Detroit, MI: Thomson Gale, 2006. Copyright © 2006 Thomson Gale. Reproduced by permission of Gale, a part of Cengage Learning.

The Development of Chronic Leukemia

Chronic leukemia is a cancer that starts in the blood cells made in the bone marrow. The bone marrow is the spongy tissue found in the large bones of the body. The bone marrow makes precursor cells called "blasts" or "stem cells" that mature into different types of blood cells. Unlike acute leukemias, in which the process of maturation of the blast cells is interrupted, in chronic leukemias, the cells do mature and only a few remain as immature cells. However, even though the cells appear normal, they do not function as normal cells.

The different types of cells that are produced in the bone marrow are red blood cells (RBCs), which carry oxygen and other materials to all tissues of the body; white blood cells (WBCs), which fight infection; and platelets, which play a part in the clotting of the blood. The white blood cells can be further subdivided into three main types: the granulocytes, monocytes, and the lymphocytes.

The granulocytes, as their name suggests, have granules (particles) inside them. These granules contain special proteins (enzymes) and several other substances that can break down chemicals and destroy microorganisms such as bacteria.

Monocytes are the second type of white blood cell. They are also important in defending the body against pathogens.

The lymphocytes form the third type of white blood cell. There are two main types of lymphocytes: T lymphocytes and B lymphocytes. They have different functions within the immune system. The B cells protect the body by making "antibodies." Antibodies are proteins that can attach to the surfaces of bacteria and viruses. This attachment sends signals to many other cell types to come and destroy the antibody-coated organism. The T cell protects the body against viruses. When a virus enters a cell, it produces certain proteins that are projected onto the surface of the infected cell. The T cells

A lab technician analyzes bone marrow samples taken from a leukemia patient in an effort to find a donor. (© **Tom Tracy Photography/ Alamy**)

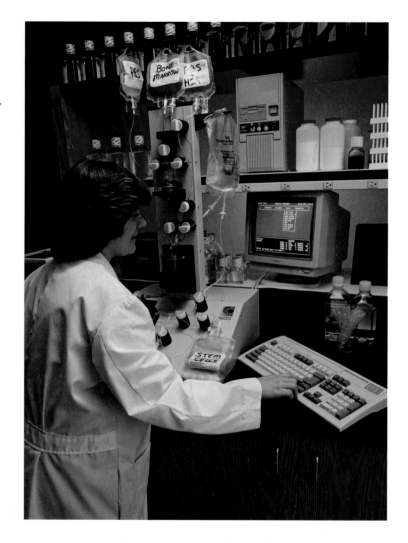

can recognize these proteins and produce certain chemicals (cytokines) that are capable of destroying the virus-infected cells. In addition, the T cells can destroy some types of cancer cells.

Chronic leukemias develop very gradually. The abnormal lymphocytes multiply slowly, but in a poorly regulated manner. They live much longer and thus their numbers build up in the body. The two types of chronic leukemias can be easily distinguished under the microscope. Chronic lymphocytic leukemia (CLL) involves the T or B lymphocytes. B cell abnormalities are more common than T cell abnormalities. T cells are affected in only 5% of the patients. The T and B lymphocytes can be differentiated from the other types of white blood cells based on their size and by the absence of granules inside them. In chronic myelogenous leukemia (CML), the cells that are affected are the granulocytes.

Chronic lymphocytic leukemia (CLL) often has no symptoms at first and may remain undetected for a long time. Chronic myelogenous leukemia (CML), on the other hand, may progress to a more acute form.

Chronic leukemias account for 1.2% of all cancers. Because leukemia is the most common form of childhood cancer, it is often regarded as a disease of childhood. However, leukemias affect nine times as many adults as children. In chronic lymphoid leukemia, 90% of the cases are seen in people who are 50 years or older, with the average age at diagnosis being 65. The incidence of the disease increases with age. It is almost never seen in children. Chronic myeloid leukemias are generally seen in people in their mid-40s. It accounts for about 40% of childhood leukemia cases. According to the estimates of the American Cancer Society (ACS), approximately 29,000 new cases of leukemia will be diagnosed in 1998.

Chronic Leukemia's Causes and Symptoms

Leukemia strikes both sexes and all ages. Although the cause is unknown, chronic leukemia is linked to genetic abnormalities and environmental factors. For example, exposure to ionizing radiation and to certain organic chemicals, such as benzene, is believed to increase the risks for getting leukemia. Chronic leukemia occurs in some people who are infected with two human retroviruses (HTLV-I and HTLV-II). An abnormal chromosome known as the Philadelphia chromosome is seen in 90% of those with CML. The incidence of chronic leukemia is slightly higher among men than women.

The symptoms of chronic leukemia are generally vague and non-specific. In chronic lymphoid leukemia (CLL), a patient may experience all or some of the following symptoms:

- swollen lymph nodes
- an enlarged spleen, which could make the patient complain of abdominal fullness
- chronic fatigue
- a general feeling of ill-health
- fever of unknown origin
- night sweats
- weight loss that is not due to dieting or exercise
- frequent bacterial or viral infections

In the early stages of chronic myeloid leukemia (CML), the symptoms are more or less similar to CLL. In the later stages of the disease, the patient may experience these symptoms:

- non-specific bone pain
- bleeding problems
- mucus membrane irritation
- frequent infections
- a pale color due to a low red blood cell count (anemia)
- swollen lymph glands
- fever
- night sweats

Diagnosis of the Disease

There are no screening tests available for chronic leukemias. The detection of these diseases may occur by chance during a routine physical examination.

If the doctor has reason to suspect leukemia, he or she will conduct a very thorough physical examination to look for enlarged lymph nodes in the neck, underarm, and pelvic region. Swollen gums, an enlarged liver or spleen, bruises, or pinpoint red rashes all over the body are some of the signs of leukemia. Urine and blood tests may be ordered to check for microscopic amounts of blood in the urine and to obtain a complete differential blood count. This count will give the numbers and percentages of the different cells found in the blood. An abnormal blood test might suggest leukemia; however, the diagnosis has to be confirmed by more specific tests.

The doctor may perform a bone marrow biopsy to confirm the diagnosis of leukemia. During the bone marrow biopsy, a cylindrical piece of bone and marrow is removed. The tissue is generally taken out of the hipbone. These samples are sent to the laboratory for examination. In addition to diagnosis, bone marrow biopsy is also done during the treatment phase of the disease to see if the leukemia is responding to therapy.

Standard imaging tests such as x rays, computed tomography scans (CT scans), and magnetic resonance imaging (MRI) may be used to check whether the leukemic cells have invaded other organs of the body, such as the bones, chest, kidneys, abdomen, or brain.

Types of Treatment

The treatment depends on the specific type of chronic leukemia and its stage. In general, chemotherapy is the standard approach to both CLL and CML. Radiation therapy is occasionally used. Because leukemia cells can spread to all the organs via the blood stream and the lymph vessels, surgery is not considered an option for treating leukemias.

Bone marrow transplantation (BMT) is becoming the treatment of choice for CML because it has the possibility of curing the illness. BMT is generally not considered an option in treating CLL because CLL primarily affects older people, who are not considered to be good candidates for the procedure.

In BMT, the patient's diseased bone marrow is replaced with healthy marrow. There are two ways of doing a bone marrow transplant. In an allogeneic bone marrow transplant, healthy marrow is taken from another person (donor) whose tissue is either the same or very closely resembles the patient's tissues. The donor may be a twin, a sibling, or a person who is not related at all. First, the patient's bone marrow is destroyed with very high doses of chemotherapy and radiation therapy. To replace the destroyed marrow, healthy marrow from the donor is given to the patient through a needle in the vein.

In the second type of bone marrow transplant, called an autologous bone marrow transplant, some of the patient's own marrow is taken out and treated with a combination of anticancer drugs to kill all the abnormal cells. This marrow is then frozen to save it. The marrow remaining in the patient's body is then destroyed with high dose chemotherapy and radiation therapy. Following that, the patient's own marrow that was frozen is thawed and given back to the patient through a needle in the vein. This mode of bone marrow transplant is currently being investigated in clinical trials.

In chronic lymphoid leukemia (CLL), chemotherapy is generally the treatment of choice. Depending on the stage of the disease, single or multiple drugs may be given. Drugs commonly prescribed include steroids, chlorambucil, fludarabine, and cladribine. Low dose radiation therapy may be given to the whole body, or it may be used to alleviate the symptoms and discomfort due to an enlarged spleen and lymph nodes. The spleen may be removed in a procedure called a splenectomy.

In chronic myeloid leukemia (CML), the treatment of choice is bone marrow transplantation. During the slow progress (chronic phase) of the disease, chemotherapy may be given to try to improve the cell counts. Radiation therapy, which involves the use of x rays or other high-energy rays to kill cancer cells and shrink tumors, may be used in some cases to reduce the discomfort and pain due to an enlarged spleen. For chronic leukemias, the

Estimated Number of New Leukemia Cases in the United States, 2007

Type	Individuals	Male	Female
Acute lymphocytic leukemia	5,200	3,060	2,140
Chronic lymphocytic leukemia	15,340	8,960	6,380
Acute myelogenous leukemia	13,410	7,060	6,350
Chronic myelogenous leukemia	4,570	2,570	2,000
Other forms of leukemia	5,720	3,150	2,570
Total	44,240	24,800	19,440

Taken from: American Cancer Society, *Cancer Facts & Figures 2007*.

source of radiation is usually outside the body (external radiation therapy). If the leukemic cells have spread to the brain, radiation therapy can be directed at the brain. As the disease progresses, the spleen may be removed in an attempt to try to control the pain and to improve the blood counts.

In the acute phase of CML, aggressive chemotherapy is given. Combination chemotherapy, in which multiple drugs are used, is more efficient than using a single drug for the treatment. The drugs may either be administered intravenously through a vein in the arm or by mouth in the form of pills. If the cancer cells have invaded the central nervous system (CNS), chemotherapeutic drugs may be put into the fluid that surrounds the brain through a needle in the brain or back. This is known as intrathecal chemotherapy.

Biological therapy or immunotherapy is a mode of treatment in which the body's own immune system is harnessed to fight the cancer. Substances that are routinely made by the immune system (such as growth factors, hormones, and disease-fighting proteins) are either synthetically made in a laboratory, or their effectiveness is boosted and they are then put back into the patient's body. This treatment mode is also being investigated in clinical trials all over the country at major cancer centers.

Prognosis and Prevention

The prognosis for leukemia depends on the patient's age and general health. According to statistics, in chronic lymphoid leukemia, the overall survival for all stages of the disease is nine years. Most of the deaths in people with CLL are due to infections or other illnesses that occur as a result of the leukemia.

In CML, if bone marrow transplantation is performed within one to three years of diagnosis, 50–60% of the patients survive three years or more. If the disease progresses to the acute phase, the prognosis is poor. Less than 20% of these patients go into remission.

Most cancers can be prevented by changes in lifestyle or diet, which will reduce the risk factors. However, in leukemias, there are no known risk factors. Therefore, at the present time, there is no way known to prevent the leukemias from developing. People who are at an increased risk for developing leukemia because of proven exposure to ionizing radiation, the organic liquid benzene, or people who have a history of other cancers of the lymphoid system (Hodgkin's lymphoma) should undergo periodic medical checkups.

An Overview of Acute Leukemias

Lata Cherath

In the following selection Lata Cherath introduces the different types of acute leukemias and discusses their symptoms, diagnoses, progression, and treatment. Cherath compares the incidence of acute lymphocytic leukemia (ALL) to acute myeloid leukemia (AML) in both children and adults. Science writer Lata Cherath was the science writing intern at the Cancer Research Institute in New York, New York, and is the editor of the *Gale Encyclopedia of Cancer.*

Leukemia is a cancer that starts in the organs that make blood, namely the bone marrow and the lymph system. Depending on their characteristics, leukemias can be divided into two broad types. Acute leukemias are the rapidly progressing leukemias, while the chronic leukemias progress more slowly. The vast majority of childhood leukemias are of the acute form.

SOURCE: Lata Cherath, *Gale Encyclopedia of Medicine.* Belmont, CA: Thomson Gale, 2006. Copyright © 2006 Thomson Gale. Reproduced by permission of Gale, a part of Cengage Learning.

Leukemia Develops in the Blood

The cells that make up blood are produced in the bone marrow and the lymph system. The bone marrow is the spongy tissue found in the large bones of the body. The lymph system includes the spleen (an organ in the upper abdomen), the thymus (a small organ beneath the breastbone), and the tonsils (an organ in the throat). In addition, the lymph vessels (tiny tubes that branch like blood vessels into all parts of the body) and lymph nodes (pea-shaped organs that are found along the network of lymph vessels) are also parts of the lymph system. The lymph is a milky fluid that contains cells. Clusters of lymph nodes are found in the neck, underarm, pelvis, abdomen, and chest.

The cells found in the blood are the red blood cells (RBCs), which carry oxygen and other materials to all tissues of the body; white blood cells (WBCs) that fight infection; and platelets, which play a part in the clotting of the blood. The white blood cells can be further subdivided into three main types: granulocytes, monocytes, and lymphocytes.

The granulocytes, as their name suggests, have particles (granules) inside them. These granules contain special proteins (enzymes) and several other substances that can break down chemicals and destroy microorganisms, such as bacteria. Monocytes are the second type of white blood cell. They are also important in defending the body against pathogens.

The lymphocytes form the third type of white blood cell. There are two main types of lymphocytes: T lymphocytes and B lymphocytes. They have different functions within the immune system. The B cells protect the body by making "antibodies." Antibodies are proteins that can attach to the surfaces of bacteria and viruses. This "attachment" sends signals to many other cell types to come and destroy the antibody-coated organism. The T cells protect the body against viruses. When a virus enters a cell, it produces certain proteins that are projected onto the surface of the infected cell. The T cells recognize these proteins and make certain chemicals that are capable of destroying the virus-infected cells. In addition, the T cells can destroy some types of cancer cells.

The bone marrow makes stem cells, which are the precursors of the different blood cells. These stem cells mature through stages into either RBCs, WBCs, or platelets. In acute leukemias, the maturation process of the white blood cells is interrupted. The immature cells (or "blasts") proliferate rapidly and begin to accumulate in various organs and tissues, thereby affecting their normal function. This uncontrolled proliferation of the immature cells in the bone marrow affects the production of the normal red blood cells and platelets as well.

A physician harvests bone marrow from a young woman's pelvis for treatment of acute leukemia. (**Dr. Rob Stepney/Photo Researchers, Inc.**)

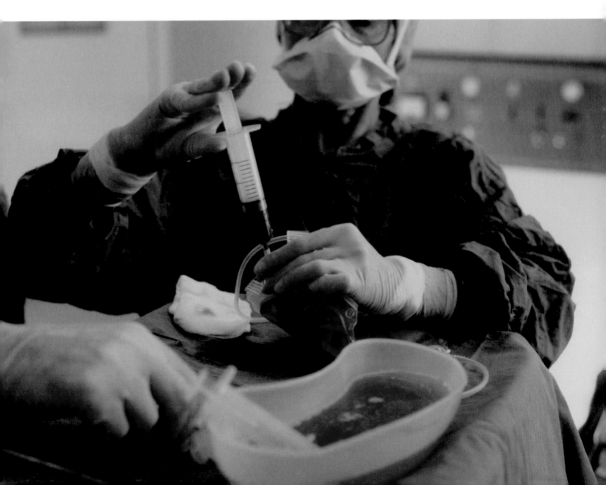

Acute leukemias are of two types: acute lymphocytic leukemia and acute myelogenous leukemia. Different types of white blood cells are involved in the two leukemias. In acute lymphocytic leukemia (ALL), it is the T or B lymphocytes that become cancerous. The B cell leukemias are more common than T cell leukemias. Acute myelogenous leukemia, also known as acute nonlymphocytic leukemia (ANLL), is a cancer of the monocytes and/or granulocytes.

Leukemias account for 2% of all cancers. Because leukemia is the most common form of childhood cancer, it is often regarded as a disease of childhood. However, leukemias affect nine times as many adults as children. Half of the cases occur in people who are 60 years of age or older. The incidence of acute and chronic leukemias is about the same. According to the estimates of the American Cancer Society (ACS), approximately 29,000 new cases of leukemia were diagnosed in 1998.

The Incidence and Symptoms of Acute Leukemia

Leukemia strikes both sexes and all ages. The human T cell leukemia virus (HTLV-I) is believed to be the causative agent for some kinds of leukemias. However, the cause of most leukemias is not known. Acute lymphoid leukemia (ALL) is more common among Caucasians than among African-Americans, while acute myeloid leukemia (AML) affects both races equally. The incidence of acute leukemia is slightly higher among men than women. People with Jewish ancestry have a higher likelihood of getting leukemia. A higher incidence of leukemia has also been observed among persons with Down syndrome and some other genetic abnormalities.

Exposure to ionizing radiation and to certain organic chemicals, such as benzene, is believed to increase the risk of getting leukemia. Having a history of diseases that damage the bone marrow, such as aplastic anemia, or a history of cancers of the lymphatic system puts people at a high risk for developing acute leukemias. Similarly, the use of anticancer medications, immunosuppressants, and the antibiotic chloramphenicol are also considered risk factors for developing acute leukemias.

The symptoms of leukemia are generally vague and non-specific. A patient may experience all or some of the following symptoms:

- weakness or chronic fatigue
- fever of unknown origin
- weight loss that is not due to dieting or exercise
- frequent bacterial or viral infections
- headaches
- skin rash
- non-specific bone pain
- easy bruising
- bleeding from gums or nose
- blood in urine or stools
- enlarged lymph nodes and/or spleen
- abdominal fullness

Diagnosing Acute Leukemia

Like all cancers, leukemias are best treated when found early. There are no screening tests available.

If the doctor has reason to suspect leukemia, he or she will conduct a thorough physical examination to look for enlarged lymph nodes in the neck, underarm, and pelvic region. Swollen gums, enlarged liver or spleen, bruises, or pinpoint red rashes all over the body are some of the signs of leukemia. Urine and blood tests may be ordered to check for microscopic amounts of blood in the urine and to obtain a complete differential blood count. This count will give the numbers and percentages of the different cells found in the blood. An abnormal blood test might suggest leukemia, however, the diagnosis has to be confirmed by more specific tests.

The doctor may perform a bone marrow biopsy to confirm the diagnosis of leukemia. During the biopsy, a cylindrical piece of bone and marrow is removed. The tissue is generally taken out of the hipbone. These samples are sent to the laboratory for examination. In addition to diagnosis, the biopsy is also repeated during the treatment phase of the disease to see if the leukemia is responding to therapy.

A spinal tap (lumbar puncture) is another procedure that the doctor may order to diagnose leukemia. In this procedure, a small needle is inserted into the spinal cavity in the lower back to withdraw some cerebrospinal fluid and to look for leukemic cells.

Standard imaging tests, such as x rays, computed tomography scans (CT scans), and magnetic resonance imaging (MRI) may be used to check whether the leukemic cells have invaded other areas of the body, such as the bones, chest, kidneys, abdomen, or brain. A gallium scan or bone scan is a test in which a radioactive chemical is injected into the body. This chemical accumulates in the areas of cancer or infection, allowing them to be viewed with a special camera.

Treatment for Leukemia

There are two phases of treatment for leukemia. The first phase is called "induction therapy." As the name suggests, during this phase, the main aim of the treatment is to reduce the number of leukemic cells as far as possible and induce a remission in the patient. Once the patient shows no obvious signs of leukemia (no leukemic cells are detected in blood tests and bone marrow biopsies), the patient is said to be in remission. The second phase of treatment is then initiated. This is called continuation or maintenance therapy, and the aim in this case is to kill any remaining cells and to maintain remission for as long as possible.

Chemotherapy is the use of drugs to kill cancer cells. It is usually the treatment of choice and is used to relieve symptoms and achieve long-term remission of the disease. Generally, combination chemotherapy, in which multiple drugs are used, is more efficient than using a single drug for the treatment. Some drugs may be administered intravenously through a vein in the arm; others may be given by mouth in the form of pills. If the cancer cells have invaded the brain, then chemotherapeutic drugs may be put into the fluid that surrounds the brain through a needle in the brain or back. This is known as intrathecal chemotherapy.

Because leukemia cells can spread to all the organs via the blood stream and lymph vessels, surgery is not considered an option for treating leukemias.

Radiation therapy, which involves the use of x rays or other high-energy rays to kill cancer cells and shrink tumors, may be used in some cases. For acute leukemias, the source of radiation is usually outside the body (external radiation therapy). If the leukemic cells have spread to the brain, radiation therapy can be given to the brain.

Bone marrow transplantation is a process in which the patient's diseased bone marrow is replaced with healthy marrow. There are two methods of bone marrow transplant. In an allogeneic bone marrow transplant, healthy marrow is taken from a donor whose tissue is either the same as or very closely resembles the patient's tissue. The donor may be a twin, a brother or sister (sibling), or a person who is not related at all. First, the patient's bone marrow is destroyed with very high doses of chemotherapy and radiation therapy. Healthy marrow from the donor is then given to the patient through a needle in a vein to replace the destroyed marrow.

In the second type of bone marrow transplant, called an autologous bone marrow transplant, some of the patient's own marrow is taken out and treated with a combination of anticancer drugs to kill all abnormal cells. This

> **FAST FACT**
>
> Blood cancers (leukemia, lymphoma, and myeloma) account for 8.7 percent of all cancer cases diagnosed in the United States each year. Every five minutes, someone is diagnosed with a blood cancer. Every ten minutes, someone dies of a blood cancer.

Approximate U.S. Prevalence of the Four Major Leukemias as of January 1, 2004

Type	Prevalence*
Chronic lymphocytic leukemia	95,579
Chronic myelogenous leukemia	21,501
Acute lymphocytic leukemia	50,189
Acute myelogenous leukemia	27,289

* Prevalence estimates are expressed here as the number of people living in whom the first involved tumor for each cancer site was diagnosed during the previous 29 years.

Taken from: *SEER (Surveillance, Epidemiology, and End Results) Cancer Statistics Review* 1975–2004, National Cancer Institute, 2007, and SEER Program.

marrow is then frozen and saved. The marrow remaining in the patient's body is destroyed with high-dose chemotherapy and radiation therapy. The marrow that was frozen is then thawed and given back to the patient through a needle in a vein. This mode of bone marrow transplant is currently being investigated in clinical trials.

Biological therapy or immunotherapy is a mode of treatment in which the body's own immune system is harnessed to fight the cancer. Substances that are routinely made by the immune system (such as growth factors, hormones, and disease-fighting proteins) are either synthetically made in a laboratory or their effectiveness is boosted and they are then put back into the patient's body. This treatment mode is also being investigated in clinical trials all over the country at major cancer centers.

Prognosis and Prevention

Like all cancers, the prognosis for leukemia depends on the patient's age and general health. According to statistics, more than 60% of of the patients with leukemia survive for at least one year after diagnosis. Acute myelocytic leukemia (AML) has a poorer prognosis rate than acute lymphocytic leukemias (ALL) and the chronic leukemias. In the last 15 to 20 years, the five-year survival rate for patients with ALL has increased from 38% to 57%.

Interestingly enough, since most childhood leukemias are of the ALL type, chemotherapy has been highly successful in their treatment. This is because chemotherapeutic drugs are most effective against actively growing cells. Due to the new combinations of anticancer drugs being used, the survival rates among children with ALL have improved dramatically. Eighty percent of the children diagnosed with ALL now survive for five years or more, as compared to 50% in the late 1970s.

Most cancers can be prevented by changes in lifestyle or diet, which will reduce risk factors. However, in leukemias, there are no such known risk factors. Therefore, at the present time, no way is known to prevent leukemias from developing. People who are at an increased risk for developing leukemia because of proven exposure to ionizing radiation or exposure to the toxic liquid benzene, and people with Down syndrome, should undergo periodic medical checkups.

A Study of Twins Helps Locate Potential Genetic Connections to Leukemia

Mark Henderson

In the following viewpoint Mark Henderson reports on researchers in Britain who are studying a set of twin girls to find genetic links to leukemia. Henderson notes that the study has explored a rare opportunity to examine twin girls who both carry genetically abnormal pre-leukemic cells. In this case, one girl developed acute lymphoblastic leukemia (ALL), while her sister remained healthy. Researchers are hoping to identify what triggers the growth of cancerous cells and why leukemia develops in some individuals but not others. Mark Henderson is a London-based science writer for the *Times*.

I dentical twin sisters have led British scientists to a breakthrough in leukaemia research that promises more effective therapies with fewer harmful side-effects.

By comparing Olivia Murphy, 4, who is in remission from acute lymphoblastic leukaemia, and her healthy

SOURCE: Mark Henderson, "Twin Girls Lead Scientists to Secret of Childhood Cancer," *The Times* (London), January 18, 2008. Reproduced by permission.

sister, Isabella, researchers have traced the tumour stem cells that drive the most common form of childhood cancer.

Chemotherapy Has Severe Effects in Young Patients

The discovery will enable doctors to screen young leukaemia patients to establish the severity of their illness and spare some the harrowing side effects of aggressive chemotherapy.

Olivia, from Bromley, southeast London, is a prime example of how hazardous this can be: although her treatment has been successful, it left her unable to fight off a chicken pox infection that blinded her in one eye.

Chemotherapy has such harsh effects on children with leukaemia that between 1 and 2 per cent die because of the drug regime, according to Philip Ancliff, the consultant who treated Olivia at Great Ormond Street Hospital in London.

The stem-cell advance, from a team led by Tariq Enver, of the University of Oxford, and Mel Greaves, of the Institute of Cancer Research in London, will also open new approaches to treating the disease more effectively. It should allow the scientists to develop ways of targeting the stem cells that drive the blood cancer and cause relapses, so that patients can be cured. This form of the disease [acute lymphoblastic leukaemia] accounts for about 85 per cent of the 450 childhood leukaemias diagnosed in Britain each year.

> **FAST FACT**
>
> If one identical twin develops childhood leukemia, the other twin has about a 20 percent chance of developing leukemia. The second twin's risk increases if the first twin's leukemia starts during the first year of life.

Researchers Identify and Study Pre-Leukaemic Cells

The study, published in *Science*, could have further implications for the cancers that cause lung and colon tumours, as these are also thought to be propagated by rogue stem cells. Another application could be preventive treatment for children like Isabella who are known to be at high risk of acute lymphoblastic leukaemia, whose "pre-leukaemic" cells could be killed before they cause any damage.

Professor Enver said: "This research means that we can now test whether the treatment of acute lymphoblastic leukaemia in children can be correlated with either the disappearance or persistence of the leukaemia stem cell. Our next goal is to target both the pre-leukaemic stem cell and the cancer stem cell itself with new or existing drugs to cure leukaemia while avoiding the debilitating and often harmful side effects of current treatments."

Professor Greaves said: "This study of a twin pair discordant for leukaemia has identified the critical stem

The study of twins' genetics has been crucial in identifying stem cells that initiate leukemia and maintain it in a covert state for several years.
(© Marvin Debinsky Photo Associates/Alamy)

cells that initiate the disease and maintain it in a covert state for several years. We suspect that these cells can escape conventional chemotherapy and cause relapse during or after treatment. These are the cells that dictate disease course and provide the bullseye to target with new therapies."

The Healthy Twin Has Pre-Leukaemic Cells

The twins have been crucial to the new research, as they are genetically identical but one has developed cancer whereas the other has not. The scientists found that the girls' blood contains genetically abnormal cells known as pre-leukaemic cells. These were formed by a mutation known as translocation, in which two genes fuse to create an abnormal new one. This random event happened in a single cell in one of the twins—it is impossible to tell which one—while they were still in the womb. As the twins shared a placenta, the original mutant's daughter cells populated the blood of both sisters.

Analysis of Isabella's blood suggests that about one in 1,000 of her lymphocyte blood cells is pre-leukaemic. About 1 per cent of these pre-leukaemic cells are also stem cells that can start and sustain the cancer.

As Isabella is still healthy, it is clear that the translocation cannot trigger leukaemia by itself. About one in 100 children has the translocation, but only one in 100 develops cancer. "The crucial question is in which cells does this start," Professor Enver said. "What is the critical hit? Isabella gave us an opportunity almost to look back in time, to see which cells the cancer begins in."

They did this by comparing the twins' blood. In Olivia, but not in Isabella, some pre-leukaemic stem cells had acquired a second genetic mutation that turned them cancerous. This could have begun in a single cell, possibly because of an infection.

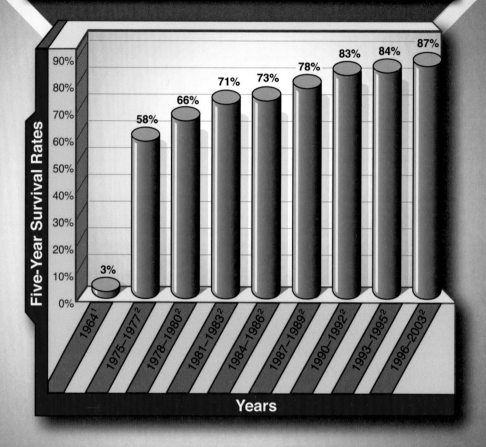

Survival Rates for Acute Lymphocytic Leukemia in Children Under 15 Years of Age

Taken from: 1. W.W. Zuelzer, "Implications of Long-Term Survivals in Acute Stem Cell Leukemia of Childhood Treated with Composite Cyclic Therapy." *Blood.* 1964:24:477–494. 2. *SEER (Surveillance, Epidemiology and End Results), Cancer Statistics Review,* 1975–2004, National Cancer Institute, 2007.

The discovery will help doctors to monitor Isabella, and children like her, so that further genetic damage in her pre-leukaemic stem cells is caught early. Her risk of acute lymphoblastic leukaemia is estimated at one in ten, compared with one in 10,000 among children with no family history. It will fall with every year that she remains healthy. By the time she is 14, her pre-leukaemic stem cells should have died naturally.

"Pre-leukaemic cells are still evident, so the sword of Damocles is still hanging there," Dr Ancliff said. "Hopefully, we will see them disappear."

The study also identifies precisely the cancerous stem cells that propagate the cancer. This should enable doctors to adjust the strength of chemotherapy to match a child's condition. As cancer stem cells can survive conventional chemotherapy, the research could also help scientists to design drugs that kill cancers.

Cancer Cluster Research May Identify Environmental Causes

Kirsten Weir

In the following selection Kirsten Weir reports on an alleged Nevada cancer cluster—a location with an abnormally high incidence of cancer. Weir discusses competing theories of what caused the high incidence of leukemia in children in Fallon, Nevada, as well as ensuing scientific investigation. Weir notes that many Fallon residents assert that pollutants from local industries are responsible for the increase in leukemia cases, but some investigators are less certain of the cancer cluster's origins. Kirsten Weir, a former *Natural History* editor, is currently a science journalist.

O n September 1, 2001, Stephanie Sands lost a two-year battle with cancer. Sands, 21, died of acute lymphocytic leukemia, a cancer of the blood and bone marrow.

Sands was living in Pennsylvania when she fell ill but had spent much of her childhood in the city of Fallon,

SOURCE: Kirsten Weir, "Cancer Cluster: Why Have So Many Children from Fallon, Nevada, Developed Cancer?" *Current Science,* vol. 93, February 1, 2008, pp. 8–12. Copyright © 2008 Weekly Reader Corporation. Reproduced by permission.

Nev. That location is significant because Sands was one of 17 children from Fallon to develop leukemia between 1997 and 2004.

Fallon is the site of a cancer cluster, a greater-than-expected number of cancer cases in a geographic area over a period of time. Now Fallon residents are demanding answers. "I am admittedly obsessed with Fallon and leukemia," Stephanie Sands's father, Floyd Sands, told the *Las Vegas Review-Journal.* Is some mysterious carcinogen (cancer-causing agent) lurking in Fallon, or has the city just been hit by random bad luck?

Countless Causes of Cancer

One in three Americans will develop some form of cancer. The causes of cancer are many, from genes to personal habits (smoking, poor diet) to environmental agents (radiation, viruses, chemicals).

Flowers left at Oats Park in Fallon, Nevada, in memoriam for the childhood cancer cluster in the town. Many residents think that it is caused by local industrial pollutants. (**AP Photo/ Joe Cavaretta**)

Identifying a single cause of any given cancer is difficult if not impossible. When a cancer cluster arises, though, epidemiologists look for something in the environment that could be involved in every case. Epidemiologists study the occurrence and distribution of diseases in a population.

Many researchers are skeptical of cancer clusters. Why? People tend to interpret random events as though they are not random. That type of false impression is called a clustering illusion. If a friend tosses a coin four times and gets four heads in a row, you might suspect him of cheating. However, four heads in a row isn't statistically unusual. In 20 flips, your friend has a 50 percent chance of getting four heads in a row. Similarly, cancer rates are naturally higher in some places and lower in others.

Joseph Wiemels, an epidemiologist at the University of California, San Francisco, believes most cancer clusters are just chance events. He says, though, "Fallon is a little different." Based on national averages, he explains, Fallon should expect about one case of childhood leukemia every three or four years. However, the small town experienced 17 cases in just a few years. "It's just too remarkable a cluster to be by chance," he says.

FAST FACT

Most United States cancer clusters involving high incidence of leukemia caused by environmental factors involve chronic exposure to benzene in the workplace and exceptionally high exposure to radiation.

Families Take Action

In the summer of 2001, Adam Jernee, 10, became the first Fallon cluster patient to die of leukemia. By then, more than a dozen cases of the disease had been diagnosed in the town. Soon after, the U.S. Centers for Disease Control and Prevention (CDC) launched an investigation. In 2003, the agency announced that it was unable to identify an environmental cause for the cluster.

The CDC might have given up, but Fallon residents weren't about to. Many united to form Families in Search of Truth. With help from Sen. Harry Reid (D-Nev.), the

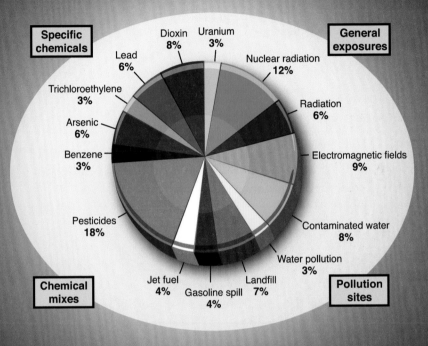

Possible Environmental Contributors to Cancer Clusters

This graph identifies the fifteen most commonly used environmental exposure terms found in articles pertaining to cancer clusters published in U.S. newspapers from 1977 to 2001.

Specific chemicals

Dioxin 8%
Uranium 3%
Lead 6%
Trichloroethylene 3%
Arsenic 6%
Benzene 3%
Pesticides 18%

General exposures

Nuclear radiation 12%
Radiation 6%
Electromagnetic fields 9%

Chemical mixes

Jet fuel 4%
Gasoline spill 4%
Landfill 7%

Pollution sites

Contaminated water 8%
Water pollution 3%

Taken from: Beverly S. Kingsley, Karen L. Schmeichel, and Carol H. Rubin, "An Update on Cancer Cluster Activities at the Centers for Disease Control and Prevention," *Environmental Health Perspectives*, January 2007. www.ehponline.org.

group secured almost $700,000 from Congress to keep funding researchers, including Wiemels and Mark Witten, of the University of Arizona College of Medicine.

Fallon is home to a number of cancer suspects, says Wiemels. "It's a hard-hit community as far as environmental issues go," he says. For starters, the town's water supply contains high levels of arsenic, a naturally occurring but poisonous element that has been linked to bladder and skin cancers, though not to leukemia.

The town also houses a U.S. Navy base with an aging jet-fuel pipeline. The fuel's chemical formula was changed in the mid-1990s, Wiemels notes, right before Fallon's kids started falling ill.

Now a third suspect has emerged. Fallon is the site of a metal refinery that processes tungsten. In its report, the CDC noted very high levels of tungsten in Fallon's drinking water. The health effects of tungsten haven't been well studied, though it has been linked to rhabdomyosarcoma (*RAB-doh-mighuh-sar-KOH-muh*), a rare cancer of connective tissue (cartilage, ligaments, muscles, and tendons).

Fallon resident Jeremy Braccini was diagnosed with leukemia at age 3. He survived but was found to have sky-high levels of arsenic and tungsten in his body. "How does a 3-year-old child get this much toxicity in his body?" his father, Jeff Braccini, asked in the *University of Nevada* magazine.

Digging for Clues

Witten is digging into the tungsten mystery. He has investigated a leukemia cluster in Sierra Vista, Ariz., and found high tungsten levels there too. Now he is researching the metal's effects on the body and plans to publish his results soon.

Tungsten may not be the only cause, though. Wiemels suspects that multiple factors have combined in Fallon to create a toxic environment that weakens the immune (disease-fighting) system.

Though teasing out the truth of the Fallon cancer cluster won't be easy, Witten is optimistic that scientists will eventually discover the cause. "I think, hopefully, we'll get to the bottom of this," he says. If he and the others can identify the true culprit, perhaps they can find a way to limit the harm it causes—not just in Fallon but everywhere. "We need to make sure our environment is as clean as we can make it so we have kids that grow up healthy," he says.

CHAPTER 2

Leukemia Issues and Controversies

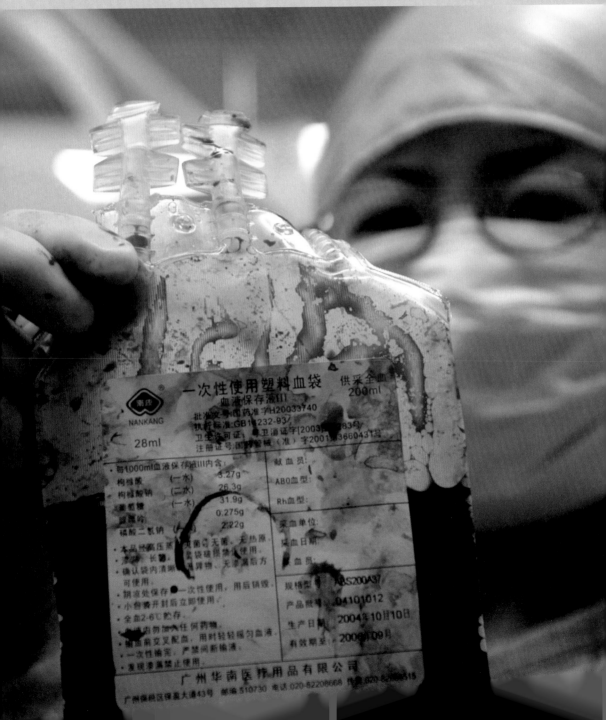

Umbilical Cord Blood Storage Holds Great Potential for Leukemia Treatment

Elizabeth Fernandez

In the following viewpoint Elizabeth Fernandez reports on several lawmakers whose experiences with leukemia inspired them to sponsor bills requiring the state of California to develop information for pregnant women about donating cord blood and laying the foundation for a public cord blood bank in the state. Former state senator Jackie Speier lost a friend to leukemia, state senator Carole Migden battled chronic myeloid leukemia (CML) herself, and state assemblyman Anthony Portantino knew a neighbor whose child received stem cells to treat leukemia. The lawmakers assert that cord blood stem cells have great medical potential and that parents should be encouraged to donate cord blood. They claim the bills' provisions will help educate people and expand access to stem cells for research and therapy. The bills were signed into law in October 2007. Elizabeth Fernandez is a reporter for San Francisco's daily newspaper, the *Chronicle*.

Photo on previous page. A technician holds umbilical cord blood collected from a newborn. Researchers hail cord blood storage as a breakthrough in leukemia treatment. (Photo by China Photos/ Getty Images)

SOURCE: Elizabeth Fernandez, "Legislators Touched by Leukemia Push Cord Blood Measures," *SF Gate*, August 13, 2007. Reproduced by permission.

For a decade, state Sen. Carole Migden quietly battled a death sentence—an unusual form of leukemia.

Now cancer-free, she wants to create a state system to collect and store umbilical cord blood, which shows enormous promise as a treatment for leukemia and other diseases.

State Assemblyman Anthony Portantino had his own brush with leukemia when a youngster on his block in his Los Angeles–area neighborhood was stricken with the disease and underwent an experimental transplant. He proposes a public cord blood collection program.

"It's a personal passion for me because a friend's life was saved," he said.

In Sacramento, umbilical cord blood has become a deeply personal issue. Behind proposed bills in both the Assembly and Senate are legislators with intimate stakes in making cord blood easier to collect and more affordable to donate, and in promoting it for medical research.

While the number of cord blood transplants nationally is growing but still relatively small, the curative powers of a newborn's umbilical stem cells remain widely untapped. According to mounting research, cord blood—which contains a cache of immature but highly adaptive cells—holds remarkable healing potential for as many as 70 blood diseases, including leukemia and sickle cell anemia.

California Legislators Advocate Cord Blood Donation

But California, unlike some other states, has no mechanism in place for a statewide public program to promote cord blood treatment and to collect donations. Private storage costs between $1,100 and $2,000 with an annual storage fee ranging from $100 to $150.

Out of 4 million births annually in the United States, the vast majority of umbilical cords are discarded.

A technician records data from umbilical cord blood storage units in China. (Xinhua/Landov)

"The science has been in place for years, but California is only now starting to catch up," said Gloria Ochoa, president of the Cord Blood Donor Foundation, a not-for-profit education program based in San Bruno. "There are about 14 other states that are proposing laws or have already passed laws to open up more public cord blood banks or to educate people about their options."

Migden and Portantino want to change the picture in California.

When a toddler up the street from Portantino's home was cured of leukemia by an experimental cord blood transplant a decade ago, Portantino became a believer. Six years later, when Portantino and his wife, Ellen, had their second daughter, they wanted to donate the cord blood.

"But I found out there was no public infrastructure," he said. "I was very frustrated. I finally found a private bank, but I had to do all the work. I said to myself, 'This is stupid. If I'm ever in a position to do anything about it, I will.' Why are we throwing it away?"

In December [2006], after being sworn into office, Portantino, D-La Cañada Flintridge (Los Angeles County), introduced his public cord blood collection measure.

"I saw Jordy grow up, I saw him at school and play, and knew his life was saved because of an umbilical cord transplant," said Portantino.

A Proposal for Research and Collection Initiatives

Migden, D-San Francisco, has proposed legislation that resonates just as strongly on a personal level. Her bill would, among other aspects, allow cord blood samples to be collected and used for medical research. It would also empower the state Department of Public Health to develop a program to collect and use cord blood.

"The application is limitless in fighting disease," Migden said. "This is an avenue that ought not to be delayed. . . . It is for every baby born in California."

Migden, 58, was diagnosed in 1997 with chronic myeloid leukemia—specialists said she had three or four years to live, five at the outside. Her options were limited: Neither of her siblings was a bone marrow match, nor was one found on a worldwide registry. For a year, Migden injected herself with interferon [proteins that assist immune response], but it proved to be a failure. So, too, was a yearlong course with an experimental drug made from the bark of a Chinese tree. Then she was accepted into an FDA [Food and Drug Administration]-funded clinical trial involving a medication called Gleevec.

> **FAST FACT**
>
> As of 2008 more than thirty-three thousand mothers have donated their infants' cord blood to the National Cord Blood Program, the world's largest public cord blood bank.

"Anybody with a time bomb gravitates toward anything that can help you," she said. The medication has since won FDA approval to treat Migden's form of the disease. "This February [2007] and again in May I was declared 100 percent clear" of cancer. "It's like a permanent remission. You take the drug every day to stay well," she said.

"A cord blood transplant wouldn't have helped me," she said. "But I got helped by something equally miraculous.

There is a miraculous aspect to cord blood. Yet it is thrown away as medical waste when it is the extreme end of everything that is not waste."

Building upon California's Prior Cord Blood Legislation

Migden's measure expands legislation by former state Sen. Jackie Speier, D-Hillsborough.

Prior to leaving office because of term limits, Speier wrote the state's first cord blood measure. It called for the state to create a public awareness campaign and to require proper licensure and regulation of cord blood banks in California. The law took effect in January [2007], but implementation has been delayed in part by the reorganization of the state Department of Health Services.

There was a deeply personal component to Speier's own legislation.

Tere Steffen, the wife of Richard Steffen, Speier's chief of staff, was diagnosed with the same unusual form of leukemia the same year that Migden was diagnosed. Tere Steffen, a Health and Welfare Agency appointee, died about five months later, leaving behind two young children.

"I saw the bill as a remarkable opportunity to do something significant in an area that had not been addressed," said Speier. "I thought it was technology that we should embrace, to make the public aware of it and to create protections necessary for public banking."

Speier also looked upon the matter from a mother's perspective. "When I gave birth in 1994 to my daughter, I cut the umbilical cord," she said. "It was such a vivid memory. I thought, 'If only I could have had the opportunity to freeze the cord blood.'"

Tere Steffen's death galvanized her husband, who has become deeply involved in promoting bone marrow donations. "Fortunately, things have occurred in the last 10 years that have made this disease more treatable," said Richard Steffen, who has held numerous influential posts

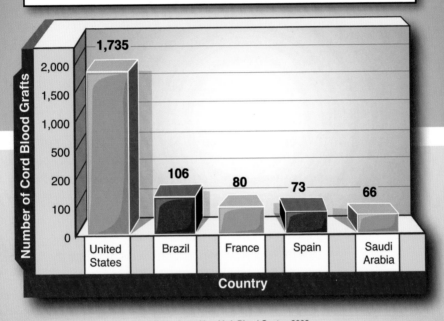

Countries with the Most Cord Blood Grafts from the New York Blood Center, 1993–2007

As of August 31, 2007, over 2,500 patients worldwide had received cord blood grafts from the New York Blood Center, one of the largest public cord blood storage banks.

Taken from: New York Blood Center, 2008.

during a long tenure at the capital, including serving as press secretary to Gov. Jerry Brown. Steffen retired in December [2006].

"The capital is no different than other businesses," he said. "It certainly has lived with cancer. It's a very supportive network; it's a place where if you have a medical need, you'll get supported."

Personal Experiences with Leukemia Spark Action

For State Auditor Elaine Howle, the disease has also hit close to home: Her confidante and legislative chief Debbie Meador was diagnosed with leukemia in April 2006.

"For me, this is not just about a professional perspective," Howle said. "It's a personal perspective. This is about somebody I care deeply about."

Since October [2006], Howle—with considerable assistance from Speier and Steffen—has organized eight bone marrow drives, including one held in her training room. [As of August 2007], 609 people have registered, about 55 percent of them minorities.

"We've heard that some matches resulted from the drives," said Howle. "It gives you the extra strength to keep doing this because you know you are saving someone's life."

Meador, who has worked in the auditor's office since 1989, is in Seattle recuperating from her second cord blood transplant. The first was in February [2007], the second in May.

"This time it worked," she said in a phone interview. "They've told me my numbers are very strong."

When Meador was diagnosed, her family was planning her 50th birthday party. The party was postponed because she was in the hospital. Then it was postponed again because she was on chemotherapy. Then she was back in the hospital.

"We're still waiting for the party," she said. "But there's no question about it, we are going to have that party."

Banking Cord Blood Has Drawbacks, Especially at Private Storage Banks

Leroy C. Edozien

Leroy C. Edozien asserts that parents of newborns should not be persuaded by health-care providers to pay for private cord blood storage. He argues that private storage is expensive and that the likelihood that the stored cells would be needed is very low. Edozien contends that many commercial storage facilities overstate the possible therapeutic uses of stem cells. Furthermore, private cord blood banking takes needed donations away from public banks that use stem cells for both research and treatment. Leroy C. Edozien is consultant obstetrician/gynecologist at St. Mary's Hospital in Manchester, England, and editor in chief of the journal *Clinical Risk*.

Storing cord blood at birth as insurance against future disease may sound like a good idea to parents, but it has worrying implications for NHS [National Health Service] services and little chance of benefit.

SOURCE: Leroy C. Edozien, "NHS Maternity Units Should Not Encourage Commercial Banking of Umbilical Cord Blood," *BMJ*, vol. 333, October 14, 2006, pp. 801–804. Copyright © 2006 BMJ Publishing Group Ltd. Reproduced by permission.

Increasing numbers of women in maternity units across the United Kingdom are requesting collection of umbilical cord blood at delivery to enable storage of stem cells for possible autologous transfusion in the future. Such commercial banking of cord blood has important implications for National Health Service maternity units. The debate on whether commercial cord blood banking should be encouraged has mostly been limited to the scientific merits, but risk management, medicolegal, and ethical issues also need considering.

Growth of Blood Banking

Umbilical cord blood is rich in stem cells that can be used to treat patients with abnormal haematopoietic [blood] cell lines, childhood leukaemia, or metabolic diseases. Bone marrow is used for this purpose, but cord blood is cheaper and easier to obtain and less likely to trigger a harmful immune response or rejection in the recipient.

For these reasons interest has been growing in banking cord blood. The collected sample is commercially processed and stored for possible autologous transfusion in the future, a practice commonly referred to as biological insurance.

Media hype about the potential of stem cell transplantation and marketing by the commercial cord blood banks are likely to increase requests for blood collection at delivery. These banks advertise on the internet, distribute literature in antenatal clinics, and directly approach doctors and midwives.

A booklet distributed by one of the commercial banks tells potential clients that, "The cure for many life threatening diseases is dependent on the transplantation of stem cells." It speaks of "unimaginable possibilities" and states: "Potentially [stem cell] research should provide answers to curing diseases such as dia-

> **FAST FACT**
>
> As of 2004 approximately 3,500 cord blood stem cell transplants in the United States were performed using cells from public banks of unrelated donors; 300 transplants used cells from sibling donors; and 14 used the patient's own cells.

betes, breast cancer, ovarian or testicular cancer, melanoma, rheumatoid arthritis, Parkinson's as well as regeneration of damaged heart tissue."

Public and Commercial Banking

The NHS has been banking donated cord blood since 1996 through designated public banks operated by the National Blood Service. Public banks collect cord blood that has been altruistically donated for haemopoietic stem cell transplantation, similar to bone marrow donation. These banks use established links with maternity units to collect cord blood on a regular basis through standard procedures and by appropriately trained staff working separately from those providing routine peripartum care.

Altruistic cord blood donations are used to treat unrelated recipients (allogeneic transplantation). Public banks also operate directed banking of cord blood in families affected by or known to be at risk of diseases that are treatable by transplanting blood stem cells. Cord blood is collected from siblings born into such families.

By contrast, commercial banks operate collection and storage of a baby's cord blood for later use by that person (autologous transplantation) or their siblings. Blood is collected just in case the baby later develops an illness such as leukaemia, which could be treated by transplantation of cord blood stem cells.

Commercial banking has been criticised by numerous medical bodies, including the Royal College of Midwives, Royal College of Obstetricians and Gynaecologists, American Academy of Pediatrics, Society of Obstetricians and Gynaecologists of Canada, American College of Obstetricians and Gynecologists, French National Consultative Ethics Committee for Health and Life Sciences, and the European Group on Ethics in Science and New Technologies. In a recently revised position paper, the Royal College of Obstetricians and Gynaecologists reaffirmed that routine directed commercial cord blood collection and stem cell storage cannot be recommended because of the insufficient scientific base and the logistic problems of collection for NHS providers.

Scientific Argument Against Commercial Banking

The advantages of commercial cord blood banking are that the child has blood stored for possible use in the future and would be able to benefit from advances in technology. The question is whether these advantages are real or hypothetical. Some scientists have tried to make a case for commercial banking based on the scientific possibilities of stem cell therapy, but most of the acclaimed benefits apply to allogeneic transplantation and not necessarily to autologous transplantation.

The scientific argument against commercial cord blood banking can be summarised as follows:

- The likelihood that the stored blood will be used is very low (estimates range from 1 in 1,400 to 1 in 20,000)
- Advances in conventional treatment and allogeneic transplantation mean only a few patients with acute leukaemia will require autologous transplantation. If autologous stem cells are required they could be harvested from bone marrow or peripheral blood
- Autologous cord blood may not be the best option— for example, pre-leukaemic mutations or leukaemic cells may be present in cord blood of children who later develop leukaemia
- Alternatives to autologous cord blood are available for people who require transplantation. These include marrow from a living related donor or cells from a matched donor from a public cord blood bank
- Arguments by commercial cord blood banks that cord blood could be used to treat diabetes and other diseases are speculative.

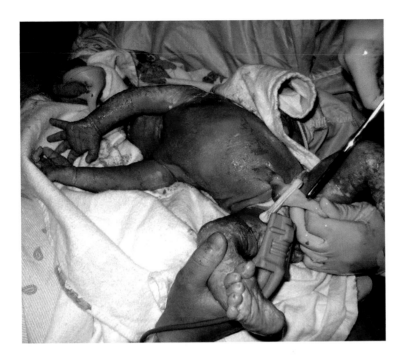

Umbilical cord blood is collected from a newborn. Stem cells taken from the blood will be used in cancer research. (**AFP/Getty Images**)

Risk Management Issues

Whatever the scientific merits or demerits, commercial collection and banking of cord blood presents many other risks that need to be taken into account. Blood can be collected from the cord while the placenta is still in utero after vaginal delivery or caesarean section (in vivo collection) or after the placenta has been delivered (in vitro collection). In vivo collection may yield larger volumes but could interfere with the mother's care—and who is to decide whether the collection takes precedence over some aspect of care: the mother or the midwife? In vitro collection increases the risk of the specimen being contaminated with bacteria or maternal fluid.

Time spent on collecting cord blood is time away from the care of this mother, the baby, and, critically, other patients, which raises ethical questions about equitable treatment of patients. Collection of cord blood could also interfere with cord blood gas analysis. Cord blood gas analysis is important in diagnosing fetal acidosis and has both clinical and medicolegal implications. What happens when samples have to be collected for both gas analysis and commercial storage? It is easy to say that the former takes priority; in practice, some parents may want it the other way.

If NHS units are to encourage commercial cord blood banking, time has to be set aside for obtaining valid consent. The consent procedure, blood collection, labelling, and associated paperwork all place an extra burden on staff. When English is not the woman's first language, a link worker will be required to obtain valid consent.

Multiple pregnancy and preterm labour create further problems. Multiple pregnancies increase the scope for error in labelling the cord blood units and for cross contamination—with serious implications for non-identical twins. . . .

Maternity units have an ethical if not legal obligation to minimise the risk of infection in cord blood units. Chorioamnionitis [infection of the placenta and amniotic fluid], genital herpes, and tears of the placental vessels due to traction all predispose to contamination, and units will have to put systems in place to pick up these risks and contain them. Ideally, the unit collecting umbilical cord blood should screen the mother for infection, including a history of overseas travel, exposure to live viral vaccines, and use of recreational drugs. These processes have resource implications that extend beyond mere collection of a sample of blood at delivery.

Concerns about quality relate not only to collection of the blood sample but also to the processing and storage of cord blood units. The European tissues and cells directive that came into force on 7 April 2006 applies to stem cells. Cord blood banks must comply with specified standards for the procurement, processing, and storage of these cells. If a maternity unit participates in the collection of cord blood it would need to meet the specified standards. Public banks have stringent quality standards, particularly in relation to infection, but in the United States private banks are reported to have lobbied hard against regulation.

These logistical problems do not apply to altruistic donation because the blood is collected by specially trained staff who are not involved in routine care and there is no imperative to obtain a sample from any particular woman. Care has to be taken to obtain valid consent, but the number of collections is contained by the available resources.

Medicolegal Issues and Ethical Considerations

Apart from consent, there are other medicolegal factors to consider. Questions arise regarding indemnity if a sample is inadequate, contaminated, or mislabelled or in any other way unsuitable for use. Are the hospital, individual practitioners, and defence organisations exempt from liability? Does collection of cord blood for commercial banking count as part of routine NHS care? If it does, is the NHS obliged to train all staff in collection, and will the cost of such training be ethically justifiable given competing claims on limited resources and cost-benefit considerations?

In addition to indemnity, issues relating to property rights over the cord blood must be considered by units collecting cord blood. The sample may be deemed to belong to the mother today (the contract is between the mother and the cord blood bank) but could the child be suing the bank or the mother for property rights to the cord blood in the future?

Legal battles are also occurring over patents. A US company is reported to have sent a letter in June 2004 warning obstetricians that collection of blood for a competitor was an infringement of patent. Although the battle has not shifted to UK courts, units wishing to collect cord blood for commercial banking must seek legal advice.

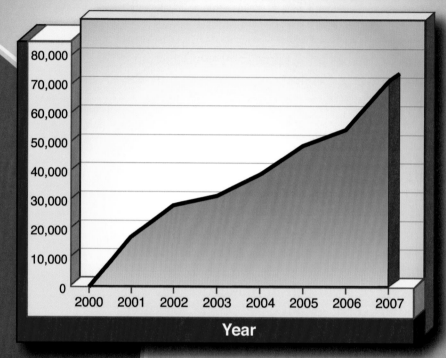

Growth of Cord Blood Units

This graph shows the growth of cord blood units on the registry of the C.W. Bill Young Cell Transplantation Program in the United States.

Year

Taken from: C.W. Bill Young Cell Transplantation Program/Bone Marrow and Cord Blood Donation and Transplantation, U.S. Department of Health and Human Services. http://bloodcell.transplant.hrsa.gov.

Some people would argue that the medical establishment's discouragement of "just in case" collection of cord blood is an extension of medical paternalism. If parents want it and can pay for it, our duty should be to provide all the information we can. The decision whether to store cord blood should be taken by parents, not by the healthcare providers. On the other hand, parents anxious to do the best they can for the unborn child are in a vulnerable position, and their autonomy is readily compromised by suggestive mailing, promotion, or advertising. Considering the stringent standards applied by ethics committees in relation to recruitment of pregnant women into research studies, it is paradoxical that when it comes to commercial cord blood banking NHS facilities could be used to promote a service that has no proved benefits.

As I have already pointed out, there are other ethical reasons not to encourage commercial cord blood banking. The idea of a midwife or doctor spending time on cord blood collection when other women need care, and in the face of a staffing (particularly midwifery) shortage, raises ethical questions. Given the logistical burden it imposes, routine on-demand collection of umbilical cord blood for commercial storage calls for dedicated resources. In the context of the NHS, such resources are better directed to meet broader and more pressing needs.

Public Policy Perspective

From the public policy perspective, it can be argued that constraining commercial cord blood banks will inhibit innovation in the science of cord blood stem cells and inhibit the growth of new biotechnology companies. This could have implications for scientific research and development and for the national economy in the long term.

The counterpoint is that promoting commercial cord blood banking would undermine the good work done by public banks. For equitable access to stem cells, altruistic donations should be encouraged. If cord blood samples are held for life in commercial banks, they are unavailable to other people who may need them. Donated samples can be traced, which means that if an altruistic donation is made and the donor subsequently needs transplantation, autologous transplantation with the donated cells may still be possible.

The balance of argument is tilted strongly against NHS trusts collecting cord blood for commercial banking. No new scientific development warrants departure from the stated positions of various medical bodies. Even if the rapid pace of technological advancement results in today's speculation becoming tomorrow's reality, risk management, medicolegal, ethical, and public policy considerations militate against commercial collection of cord blood in NHS maternity units. It should therefore be NHS policy not to facilitate umbilical cord blood collection by its staff.

Women will continue to request such collection, and it is our responsibility to provide them with adequate information explaining why commercial banking is not encouraged. As well as being given a realistic assessment of the value of cord blood banking, parents need to know how their care, and the care of other women, can be affected by cord blood collection and what could go wrong during collection. Maternity units should produce patient information leaflets providing evidence based information on this subject, as recommended by the royal colleges.

Breast-Feeding May Lower the Risk of Childhood Leukemia

Women's Health Weekly

The following viewpoint reports on a 2004 review of studies conducted from 1988 to 2003 that linked the routine breast-feeding of infants with a lower risk of childhood acute leukemias. The report claims that breast-feeding allows a mother to pass on antibodies that may block a necessary genetic trigger for leukemia. The report asserts that even short-term breast-feeding (three to six months) may have some leukemia-preventing benefits. *Women's Health Weekly* is a weekly Internet digest and newsletter, published since 1994, that provides summaries of major research reports and findings on women's health issues.

B abies who are breastfed have a lower risk of developing childhood leukemia, according to a new analysis of 14 studies by researchers at the University of California [UC], Berkeley.

The paper, published in the November 2004 issue of *Public Health Reports*, found that breastfeeding was

linked to lower risks of both acute lymphoblastic leukemia (ALL), the most common of the childhood cancers, and acute myeloblastic leukemia (AML).

"Our paper is the first to systematically review the epidemiologic evidence of the link between maternal breastfeeding and the risk of childhood leukemia," said Marilyn Kwan, UC Berkeley post doctoral researcher in epidemiology at the School of Public Health and lead author of the study. "We conducted this meta-analysis because the studies that had been conducted previously have been inconclusive and contradictory. Our review of the scientific literature shows that the evidence is definitely pointing towards the benefits of breastfeeding when it comes to the risk for two kinds of childhood leukemia, ALL and AML."

The 14 case-control studies, taken from around the world, were published between 1988 and 2003. They included 6,835 cases of ALL and 1,216 cases of AML.

The Possible Causes of Childhood Leukemia

While the causes of childhood leukemia are not completely understood, it is believed that the disease begins with a genetic change that occurs while the fetus is in the womb. This theory is supported by researchers, led by Mel Greaves of London's Institute of Cancer Research, who studied blood samples taken at birth and found the presence of an abnormal fusion of two genes, TEL and AML1. The cause of the gene fusion is not certain, said Kwan, but it has been shown to interfere with the normal formation and development of blood cells in animals and is found in 25% of children with leukemia.

The genetic abnormality does not guarantee that a child will go on to develop leukemia, said the researchers. Studies indicate that only 1 in 100 children with the gene fusion at birth go on to develop the disease.

"The gene fusion in and of itself doesn't cause leukemia," said Kwan. "There needs to be a second promoting step, a rare response in the child to early infections that can cause a secondary genetic change. That's where breastfeeding may come into play. It could be preventing that second event from occurring because the mother is passing along her antibodies to the child through her breast milk and strengthening the baby's immune system."

According to the U.S. National Cancer Institute, leukemia is the leading cause of cancer deaths in the United States among children younger than 15. From 1975 through 1995, ALL accounted for 78% of U.S. childhood leukemia cases, while AML accounted for 16% of cases. The bone marrow of both ALL and AML patients produces too many immature cells that fail to develop into mature white blood cells.

One of the 14 papers reviewed at UC Berkeley included a small case-control study authored by Kwan as part of the Northern California Childhood Leukemia Study. That study was funded by the U.S. National Institute of

Environmental Health Sciences and led by Patricia Buffler, a UC Berkeley professor of epidemiology who also is co author of the analysis.

Breastfeeding May Lower Risk of Childhood Leukemia

Encouragingly, the analysis indicates that even short-term breastfeeding, for less than 6 months, was linked to a lower risk of ALL.

"Our data suggest that breastfeeding for even a short period of time is protective," said Buffler.

"That's actually not surprising. We know that much of the protection provided by maternal antibodies comes in the first couple of months of breastfeeding, so even breastfeeding for 3 months is beneficial."

The researchers found no significant association between short-term breastfeeding and AML.

While the classification of ALL in the analysis is straightforward, the researchers pointed out that the classification of AML is more variable. Four of the 14 studies specified "other leukemia" or "acute non-lymphoblastic leukemia," which the researchers categorized as AML since it represents the majority of non-ALL cases. However, the researchers acknowledged that the classification method somewhat limits the conclusions they can draw about the impact of breastfeeding on AML.

In addition, they noted the inherent limitations of the case-control studies in the meta-analysis. The people in control groups in such studies tend to have a higher socio-economic status than those in case groups, the researchers said. They say that people of higher socio-economic status tend to be more educated about health issues and more willing to participate in epidemiological studies.

> **FAST FACT**
>
> A 2006 U.S. survey indicated that 77 percent of new mothers breast-fed their infants. Over half of the surveyed mothers cited "health benefits" (for infant and mother) as a primary motivation for breast-feeding.

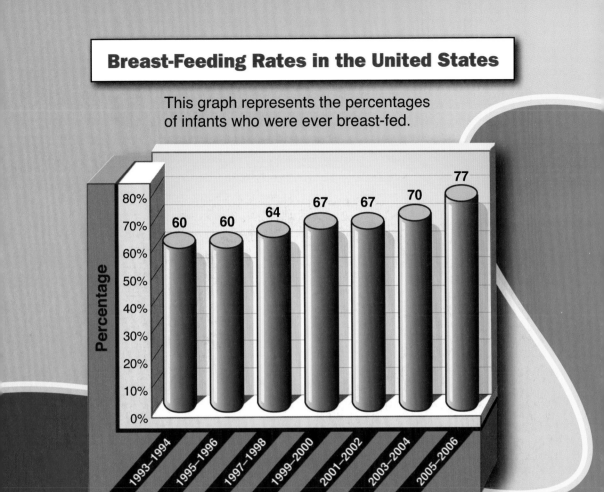

Breast-Feeding Rates in the United States

This graph represents the percentages of infants who were ever breast-fed.

Percentage

80%	
70%	60 60 64 67 67 70 77
60%	
50%	
40%	
30%	
20%	
10%	
0%	

1993–1994 1995–1996 1997–1998 1999–2000 2001–2002 2003–2004 2005–2006

Taken from: CDC/NCHS National Health and Nutrition Examination Survey, 2006.

They add that women with a higher socio-economic status also tend to report higher rates of breastfeeding.

The researchers said that larger cohort studies [of infants born within a particular period of time] are needed to determine whether breastfeeding truly has a protective effect on childhood leukemia risk.

Reasearchers Recommend Breastfeeding

One such cohort study may be the U.S. National Children's Study, which examines the environmental influences on the health and development of more than

100,000 children across the United States. Participants in the study will be followed from birth until age 21. Preliminary results of the study are expected as early as 2008.

Nevertheless, authors of the meta-analysis said there is now enough evidence on the reduced risk of childhood leukemia to recommend breastfeeding. They also cited the other health benefits breastfeeding imparts to the child.

"The overall risk of a child developing leukemia is relatively small, so based upon this analysis, people shouldn't be made to feel guilty if they can't breastfeed," said Vincent Kiley, a pediatric oncologist with Kaiser Permanente and coauthor of the paper. "But if you're on the fence about it, this study provides one more reason to encourage women to breastfeed, even if it is for just a couple of months."

Conceiving Children as Potential Cord Blood Donors Is Controversial

Peter Gorner

In the following viewpoint Peter Gorner reports on the growing number of families choosing to have another child in order to find a matching donor for an ill child. Parents are able to genetically screen embryos and select those best suited to be matching stem cell or organ donors. Some observers claim that genetically selecting embryos for donor compatibility, and having one child to save another, raises ethical concerns. Gorner reports that matched siblings could feel pressure to donate later in life should their sibling's illness return, or that individuals may someday begin to use genetic screening of embryos to select for superficial—not medical or lifesaving—characteristics such as eye color. A Pulitzer prize–winning science journalist, Peter Gorner wrote for the *Chicago Tribune* for over forty years.

Genetic testing of embryos outside the womb has led to the births of five babies selected to produce umbilical cord blood or bone marrow to save the lives of seriously ill siblings, Chicago doctors reported [in May of 2004].

SOURCE: Peter Gorner, "Five Babies Born to Save Siblings, Doctors Say," *Chicago Tribune*, May 5, 2004. Reproduced by permission.

Infusion of cord blood, a procedure similar to a bone marrow transplant, has so far put one sibling's leukemia into remission, the scientists reported in the *Journal of the American Medical Association.*

Cord blood specialist Dr. John Wagner holds Adam, the brother of Molly Nash (left). Molly received a transplant from Adam's umbilical cord blood, and her blood and bone marrow now carry Adam's cells. (**Photo by Mark Engebretson for the University of Minnesota/ Getty Images**)

The controversial procedure, which employs cutting-edge genetic tests during in-vitro fertilization, expands the possibilities of the creation of so-called "savior babies" to provide stem cells for older children who lack compatible donors for bone marrow transplants.

The procedure raises questions among ethicists, but is backed by public opinion. In the largest survey about pre-implantation genetic testing so far, researchers at Johns Hopkins University found 61 percent of the public embraces the idea of using the tests to select an embryo that could benefit an ailing sibling.

Scientists at the Reproductive Genetics Institute . . .
reported the first use of the technique to test tissue compatibility in embryos.

The Process of Transplantation

After eggs are removed from women and fertilized with
the husband's sperm, they are tested for genes that make
antigens, which tell the body whether transplanted tissue is "self" or "non-self" and should be rejected. These
antigens—known as HLA [human leukocyte antigen]—
are proteins on the surface of body cells that give the immune system a way to determine what belongs
in the body and what does not. Matching antigens will permit the body to accept a transplant
and not reject it.

Compatible embryos are then transferred
back into the womb in the hopes that at least
one will implant in the uterus and a pregnancy will develop. At the time of publication, the
Chicago scientists were able to create babies for
five of nine couples whose other children already suffered from bone marrow failure.

> **FAST FACT**
>
> Based on 2002–2003
> data, one in seventy-nine people will be diagnosed with leukemia
> during their lifetime.

The affected youngsters have acute lymphoid leukemia, acute myeloid leukemia or the rare blood disorder
Diamond-Blackfan anemia, diseases that require antigen-matched stem cell transplantation.

Umbilical cord blood from one of the babies already
has saved a sibling, another transplant is pending, and
three of the affected children were in remission and may
need the stem cell transplants later, the scientists said.

Thousands of children die each year because matching donors for bone marrow transplants can't be found.
Genetic testing of embryos may offer the last resort for
couples who want to have another child who is healthy
and can perhaps also save the life of a sibling.

"Screening embryos for compatibility is still highly
controversial and even not allowed in some countries, but

it appears to be a reasonable option for couples," said the institute's director, Yury Verlinsky, who has pioneered the field of preimplantation genetic diagnosis, or PGD. "Desperate people are getting pregnant and terminating pregnancies because the baby would have the wrong [antigen] type. With this technique they can create a baby that's compatible and save the stem cells for the victim."

Embryo Selection and Transplantation Successes

In the past, Verlinsky gained worldwide publicity for doing genetic testing that led to the birth of Adam Nash, who saved his sister, Molly, from dying of the lethal genetic blood disease Fanconi anemia.

The institute also gained considerable publicity for creating the first baby to be born free of a severe and often lethal birth defect and a healthy baby girl who was born without the gene that is causing early-onset Alzheimer's disease in her mother, as well as children who escaped inherited predispositions to many forms of cancer that may not show up until adulthood.

In an editorial accompanying the report Tuesday, Dr. Norman C. Fost, a pediatrics professor and the director of the bioethics program at the University of Wisconsin, favored the use of the technology to test compatibility for transplantation.

"In all other cases, PGD was used to make sure a baby did not have some serious genetic disorder that runs in the family. What's new here is that the older children have diseases, like leukemia, with no known genetic causes. So the point of PGD is to select embryos of the same tissue type. In some of these PGD families, cord blood may work, but months or years later the bone marrow supply may slowly die out and another transplant would be needed. So there's some chance these children could be bone marrow donors."

Ethical objections about bone marrow donation are not sufficient to prohibit families from getting this kind of assistance, Fost said. "It offers the opportunity to save the life of an existing child with an otherwise untreatable disorder and allows couples to avoid confronting the difficulties of prenatal diagnosis for [antigen] typing in mid-pregnancy, with selective abortion of fetuses who are poorly matched with the affected child," he wrote in *JAMA* [*Journal of the American Medical Association*].

Two Possible Problems

Another expert, Arthur L. Caplan, director of the Center for Bioethics at the University of Pennsylvania, has followed the work of Verlinsky and other PGD innovators with interest. "The two key issues I see are the possible health risks of embryo biopsy and testing to any children made via PGD—that is unknown at this time and it's not clear what follow-up is going on with PGD babies by

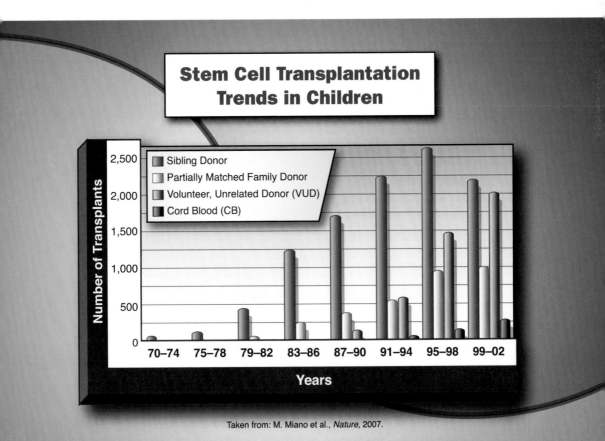

Taken from: M. Miano et al., *Nature*, 2007.

Yury [Verlinsky] or anyone else. The second problem is the presumption that you must donate tissue if you are made to be a match."

Stem cells from cord blood are no problem, Caplan said, but the matching sibling could face pressures later in life that are not consistent with donor ethics of organs and tissues. "That said, I don't think this practice should be banned. I am more concerned about proper counseling for parents who are thinking about going this route by someone other than the purveyor of the technology."

Verlinsky wrote that he assembled a large and diverse board of volunteers, independent of his institute, who studied the ethics and approved of the procedure before he attempted it.

To test the embryos, DNA was removed following in-vitro fertilization and analyzed for antigen genes to determine if the embryo's genes matched those of the sibling.

The testing required a total of 199 eight-celled embryos, many of which lost the luck of the draw merely because they weren't compatible. Verlinsky said the loss was preferable to aborting fetuses for the same reason. "I don't think many of our clients are creating a second baby just for treatment," he said. "They want to have another baby. A healthy one. But on top of that, they now have a way of saving the child who's sick."

The public apparently agrees, but still has concerns, according to a survey. . . .

"There is strong support for using these technologies when there is a health benefit, even when that benefit is for another person," said Kathy Hudson, founder and director of the Johns Hopkins University Genetics and Public Policy Center. "But this support coexists with deep-seated worries about where all these technologies may be taking us. For example, 80 percent of respondents were concerned that if not regulated, reproductive genetics technologies such as PGD could get 'out of control.'"

Benefits of Genetically Screened "Donor Children" Outweigh Ethical Concerns

ABC News

In the following selection ABC News features stories of several families who stand by their decision to use genetic screening to help conceive donor children. The parents profiled assert that their donor children were wanted and loved in their own right, not just for their potential to provide stem cells, marrow, or organs to their ill siblings. These families claim that genetic screening helped them not only to save a child, but also to ensure that future children were free of the illness. ABC News is one of the major television network news broadcasters in the United States.

Most parents would do anything to keep their children safe. But what can parents do when their child is sick with a deadly disease and requires a bone marrow transplant?

Many in this situation are turning to a controversial procedure in which they choose to have another baby

SOURCE: "Save a Dying Child: Have Another One," ABC News, November 6, 2007. Reproduced by permission.

genetically selected from embryos created outside the womb to save the life of their sick child.

The following are several stories of families who made the choice to have a genetically selected baby to save their child's life.

The Elisabeth Hartmann Story

When Elisabeth Hartmann was 10 years old, she got a baby brother named Michael who literally saved her from death.

Elisabeth was dying of a disease called Fanconi anemia that wasn't letting her body make healthy blood. "She had very little time left," her father, John, told ABC News.

Elisabeth needed a bone marrow transplant. "Without treatment she would have died," Elisabeth's mom, Martina, said.

The best option for Elisabeth's survival were stem cells from a close genetic match. And that's what Michael delivered just in time by being born.

"I held the umbilical cord, and [the doctor] milked it into a small, little cup that I was holding, so we could gather this 1 or 2 ounces of precious blood," John said.

But the fact that the blood from Michael's cord was able to save his sister is no accident, because Michael was no accident. He was genetically selected for birth from more than 40 embryos his parents conceived outside the womb using a process called preimplantation genetic diagnosis.

Dr. John Wagner, director of the Division of Hematology-Oncology and Blood and Marrow Transplantation at the University of Minnesota, pioneered the procedure in which a mother is given fertility drugs to make an increased amount of eggs to better the odds of creating an embryo with the right DNA.

Michael was chosen for life over more than 40 other potential siblings because he had what his family needed.

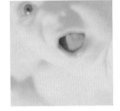

A poster from the Genetic Disease Foundation touts that one genetic screening test can identify up to eleven genetic diseases. **(Photo by Business Wire via Getty Images)**

The "unchosen" remain in deep freeze or were donated for research.

John Hartmann acknowledges the ethics of choosing which embryo will be born can be debated. "If you have a dying child, I'm not saying it's OK to do anything, but I think it's OK to use reasonable ethical measures to save your child's life," he said of his family's decision.

But Michael is loved just for being Michael, though his parents know that if they hadn't had Michael, they'd no longer have Elisabeth.

The Molly Nash Story

John and Lisa Nash knew something was wrong as soon as their daughter, Molly, was born. Before they even held their newborn baby, doctors whisked her away.

Molly had no thumbs, no hip sockets, two holes in her heart and was deaf in one ear.

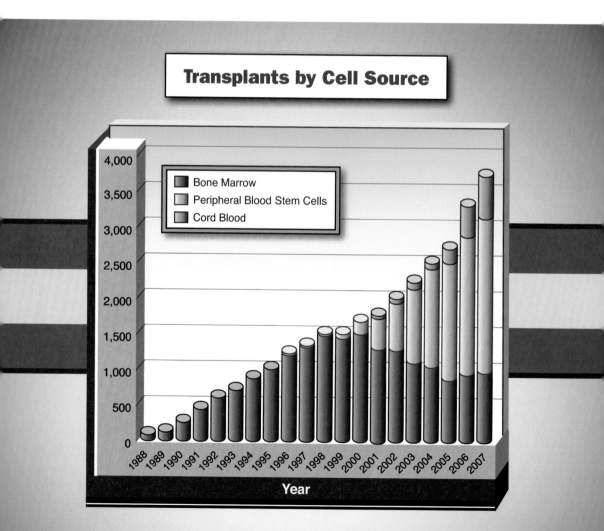

Transplants by Cell Source

- Bone Marrow
- Peripheral Blood Stem Cells
- Cord Blood

Year

Taken from: C.W. Bill Young Cell Transplantation Program/National Bone Marrow Donor Registry.

She was afflicted with the same disease as Elisabeth Hartmann, Fanconi anemia. In Molly's case, the disease would likely lead to bone marrow failure and leukemia. She was not expected to live past the age of 10.

Caring for Molly grew increasingly difficult for her parents. Her disease caused severe digestive problems for Molly, who had trouble eating without vomiting. Doctors had to put a feeding tube in her and perform multiple surgeries on her hands to make them functional.

When Molly was about 3½ years old, her bone marrow started to fail. A bone marrow transplant seemed impossible when a matching donor could not be found. "We were so brokenhearted, and I really was scared that Molly might not live," Lisa told ABC News' "20/20" in 2001.

Then Wagner told the Nashes of his procedure that could save Molly's life, and the Nashes chose to have a baby that was genetically selected to match Molly's bone marrow. As the couple struggled to conceive the genetically selected baby through in vitro fertilization, Molly's condition took a turn for the worse.

> **FAST FACT**
>
> In the United States approximately twenty thousand leukemia patients require a transplant, but only 20 percent of those will have a matching sibling donor.

"She was now starting to require transfusions, her blood counts were such that she was very prone to developing an overwhelming infection at any time . . . we were at the very bottom of what we could tolerate," Wagner said on "20/20."

Finally Lisa conceived a son that would be able to help Molly. "I started screaming and crying. I told Molly she was going to have a brother," she said.

After the baby, Adam, was born, doctors took blood from the placenta. It was given to Molly and ended up saving her life.

Adam was the first child born using this procedure, and many people debated whether the Nashes chose to "play God" when having Adam for the purpose of saving Molly's life.

"God gave us this technology. If God did not want [preimplantation genetic diagnosis] to be available, he would not have allowed the doctors to figure out how to do this," Lisa said.

The Anissa Ayala Story

Some parents have tried to conceive a child to help their other sick children without the help of treatments like preimplantation genetic diagnosis.

Abe and Mary Ayala made headlines in the early 1990s when they went public with their intentions to have a third child in the hopes of producing a bone marrow match for their middle child. The Ayalas' daughter, Anissa, had myelogenous leukemia, and a suitable donor could not be found.

Both over the age of 40, Abe reversed the vasectomy he had received nearly two decades earlier and Mary conceived with the hope that their new baby would beat the one in four odds and be a match for Anissa.

Abe told The Associated Press that if it weren't for his daughter's illness, "we would have never had another baby this late."

Luckily for the Ayalas, the new baby was a match for Anissa's bone marrow. Fourteen months after she was born, baby Marissa's bone marrow was given to her older sister, saving her life.

Abe and Mary's decision to conceive Marissa solely for the purpose of saving their other daughter's life created ethical debates across the country. After the transplant, the sisters appeared on the June 17, 1991, cover of *Time* and were the subject of the 1993 TV movie *For the Love of My Child: The Anissa Ayala Story.*

Now 35, Anissa recognizes the special bond her parents' decision created between her and Marissa. "What they did was really, completely just a blessing," she told *Newsday.* "My sister is the one who will tell you that without me she wouldn't be here, and without her, I wouldn't be here."

Artificial Sweeteners May Increase Leukemia Risk

Daniel J. DeNoon

In the following viewpoint Daniel J. DeNoon reports on a study linking consumption of artificial sweeteners to leukemia and other blood cancers. The Italian study found a high incidence of blood cancers in a population of lab rats given high doses of common artificial sweeteners. Artificial sweeteners, also called sugar substitutes, are found in many everyday products, from diet sodas to cough medicines. While researchers admit the possible risk to humans is small, and not well studied, they still advise people to limit their intake of products with artificial sweeteners. Daniel J. DeNoon is a senior medical writer for WebMD, an Internet clearinghouse of medical and health information.

A study of rats links low doses of aspartame—the sweetener in NutraSweet, Equal, and thousands of consumer products—to leukemia and lymphoma. But food industry officials point out that many other studies have found no link between aspartame and cancer.

SOURCE: Daniel J. DeNoon, "Study Links Aspartame to Cancer: Lymphoma, Leukemia in Rats Fed Sweetener; Some Dispute Results," CBSNews.com, July 28, 2005. Reproduced by permission.

The Context of the Study

The rats in the study were fed various doses of aspartame throughout their lives. In female but not male rats, lymphoma and leukemia were significantly associated with daily aspartame doses as low as 20 milligrams (mg) per kilogram (kg) of body weight. And there was a trend toward these cancers at doses as low as 4 mg/kg of body weight.

Although researchers admit that the possible risk to people is low and not well studied, they still advise people to limit their intake of artificial sweeteners. (AP Photo/ Winslow Townson)

To reach a dose of 20 mg/kg, a 140-pound woman would need to drink three cans of diet soda a day. A 180-pound man would need to drink four cans of diet soda a day.

And diet soda isn't the only source of aspartame. The sweetener is in thousands of products, ranging from yogurt to over-the-counter medicines.

The average person consumes about 2 or 3 mg/kg aspartame each day. However, that figure goes way up for children and young women.

The study comes from an independent research team led by Morando Soffritti, MD, scientific director of the European Ramazzini Foundation of Oncology and Environmental Sciences in Bologna, Italy. "What I am recommending is for healthy children and women—if they do not have diabetes—to avoid consumer use of aspartame," Soffritti tells WebMD. "We cannot continue to use aspartame in 6,000 types of products, soft drinks, yogurt, and whatever."

Consumer Group Reacts

A consumer watchdog group, the Center for Science in the Public Interest [CSPI], has called for FDA [Food and Drug Administration] action. At a minimum, the FDA should start its own studies and warn consumers of the potential danger, says CSPI Executive Director Michael F. Jacobson, PhD.

"The U.S. government really should analyze this study very carefully. If it is accepted as top quality, it could lead to a ban on aspartame," Jacobson tells WebMD. "I think a lot of companies are going to see the writing on the wall from this study and switch to newer artificial sweeteners. Meanwhile, I think consumers should switch to Splenda, the sweetener known as sucralose."

But Jacobson urges consumers not to panic. "The risk to an individual is quite small," he says. "So people

> **FAST FACT**
>
> The U.S. National Cancer Institute (NCI) estimates that incidence of cancer could be dramatically reduced—as much as 80 percent—by addressing environmental causes such as radiation and hazardous chemical exposure, pollution, tobacco, alcohol, and diet.

shouldn't fear that if they have one diet soda a day they are going to develop cancer. And I must say, the one qualm I have about the study is they found an increased risk of cancer at such a low level of exposure. If aspartame were that potent a carcinogen, I wonder if we wouldn't be seeing a real epidemic of cancer."

Soffritti has presented his findings to the European Food Safety Authority [EFSA]. In its 2002 review of aspartame safety, the EFSA found no cause for alarm. It promises that the new data will get a "high priority" evaluation.

"EFSA does not consider it appropriate to suggest any change in consumers' diets relative to aspartame on the basis of the information it currently has," the EFSA announced on July 14 [2005].

The Low-Calorie Industry Asserts the Safety of Aspartame

The new findings fly in the face of all previous studies of aspartame safety, says the Calorie Control Council [CCC], an international association representing the low-calorie and reduced-fat food and beverage industry.

The Soffritti study findings "are not consistent with the extensive scientific research and regulatory reviews done on aspartame," the CCC says in a statement. "Aspartame has been used by hundreds of millions of consumers around the world for over 20 years. With billions of man-years of safe use, there is no indication of an association between aspartame and cancer in humans." The CCC points to four long-term studies on aspartame that failed to find any relationship between aspartame and any form of cancer.

It's true that reports linking brain and breast cancer to aspartame had little merit, says blood-cancer specialist Martin R. Weihrauch, MD, of the University of Cologne, Germany. [In 2004], Weihrauch reported on his analysis of all published studies on artificial sweeteners in the *Annals of Oncology*. "The entire stuff about brain tumors and breast cancer was really nonsense," Weihrauch tells WebMD.

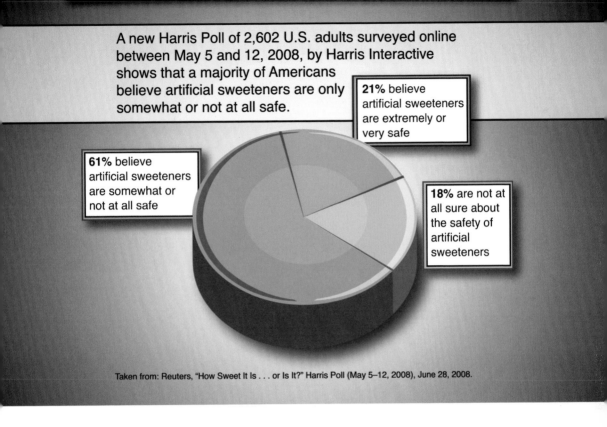

The Majority of Americans Think Artificial Sweeteners Are Somewhat or Not at All Safe

A new Harris Poll of 2,602 U.S. adults surveyed online between May 5 and 12, 2008, by Harris Interactive shows that a majority of Americans believe artificial sweeteners are only somewhat or not at all safe.

21% believe artificial sweeteners are extremely or very safe

61% believe artificial sweeteners are somewhat or not at all safe

18% are not at all sure about the safety of artificial sweeteners

Taken from: Reuters, "How Sweet It Is . . . or Is It?" Harris Poll (May 5–12, 2008), June 28, 2008.

So what does he think of the new study linking aspartame to leukemia and lymphoma? "I think it is shocking news," he says. "However, the data have to be carefully reviewed and the study redone. Not because of their methods, probably they are fine. But for a study like this, which brings out data that would make a big change in what consumers do every day, it certainly has to be confirmed. It is worrisome."

What Happened to the Rats

Soffritti's study findings may be a first report, but the study was quite thorough. It looked at 1,800 rats fed various doses of aspartame—or no aspartame at all—from age 8 weeks until death. When the animals died, the researchers did a thorough autopsy.

They found that:

- A daily dose of 20 milligrams of aspartame per kilogram of body weight was linked to lymphomas and leukemias in female—but not male—rats.
- Rats that got daily doses of as little as 4 mg/kg aspartame got lymphomas and leukemias 62% more often than those that got no aspartame, but this finding could have been due to chance.
- A few brain tumors were seen in rats fed aspartame, while those who did not get the sweetener did not get brain tumors. But this finding, too, could have been due to chance.

Artificial Sweeteners Are Not Linked to Leukemia Risk

National Cancer Institute, National Institutes of Health

The National Cancer Institute conducted a study in 2006 to assess whether consuming artificial sweeteners raised one's risk of leukemias and other cancers. The study looked at groups of people who consumed diet sodas containing aspartame, a popular artificial sweetener, and concluded that the sweetener was most likely not linked to increased cancer risk. The study findings, presented here in a question-and-answer format, note that it evaluated only moderate or average consumption of artificially sweetened beverages. The National Cancer Institute, part of the U.S. National Institutes of Health, coordinates the National Cancer Program, which conducts, coordinates, and supports cancer education, research, training, and other programs.

W*hy was an aspartame study initiated?*
Researchers from the National Cancer Institute (NCI) initiated this research because an earlier study showed that female rats fed the artificial sweetener aspartame developed more lymphomas and

SOURCE: "Aspartame and Cancer: Questions and Answers," National Cancer Institute, www.cancer.gov, September 12, 2006.

leukemias than rats that received no aspartame in their feed. The risk of cancer in that study grew with the increased amount of aspartame given to the rats. Some of the dosages may have been relevant to human intake (as low as 20 milligrams per kilogram of body weight, which would be equivalent to a 165-pound person consuming about eight cans of diet soda).

Other questions regarding the safety of aspartame were raised by a 1996 report suggesting that an increase in the number of people with brain tumors between 1975 and 1992 might be associated with the introduction and use of this sweetener in the United States. However, this report was later criticized by the scientific community for committing "ecological fallacy". Ecological fallacy refers to making a wrong conclusion about cause and effect in one person based on collection of data from a group of people; i.e., relating two things that happen at the same time, such as aspartame use and an increase in the number of brain cancer cases seen in a population, without examining whether individuals who consume aspartame also develop brain cancer.

A New Study Is Conducted

What did the researchers find in this current study?

Researchers examined the consumption of aspartame-containing beverages among the participants of the NIH-AARP [National Institutes of Health—American Association of Retired Persons] Diet and Health Study and reported that, in a comparison of people who drank aspartame-containing beverages with those who did not, increasing levels of consumption were not associated with an increased risk of lymphomas, leukemias, or brain cancers in men or women.

An increase in cancer risk was not found for the main subtypes of lymphoid cancers (Hodgkin lymphoma, non-Hodgkin lymphoma, and multiple myeloma), non-

Hodgkin lymphoma subtypes (including small lymphocytic lymphoma and chronic lymphocytic leukemia, immunoblastic lymphoma and lymphoblastic lymphoma/leukemia), or non-lymphoid leukemias.

How was the study done?

NCI researchers examined data from the NIH-AARP Diet and Health Study to investigate questions about aspartame and risk for lymphoma, leukemia, and brain cancers. The NIH-AARP Diet and Health Study is an observational study where people provide information on a questionnaire about their recent intake of various foods

The National Cancer Institute conducted studies that concluded that artificial sweeteners in diet soda are most likely not linked to cancer risk. (© BananaStock/ **SuperStock**)

and then are followed up for subsequent development of cancer. Specifically, about half a million AARP members (285,079 men and 188,905 women) who were 50 to 71 years old and living in eight study areas across the U.S. were given a questionnaire in 1995 and 1996. The participants were followed until the end of 2000 by linkage of their records with cancer registries that track the occurrence of new cancers.

The questionnaire inquired about consumption frequency and diet drink-type preference for three potentially aspartame-containing beverages (soda, fruit drinks, and iced tea), as well as aspartame added to coffee and hot tea. The researchers then computed daily consumption of aspartame, taking into account aspartame content, portion size, and consumption frequency of each beverage. The estimated aspartame intake was next compared with the occurrence of 1,888 lymphomas or leukemias and 315 malignant brain cancers to see if there was any correlation between intake and cancer.

What is the significance of the current study?

As the largest study of diet and cancer to date in the U.S., the NIH-AARP Diet and Health Study allowed researchers to examine even relatively rare cancers and their subtypes. The information on people's food consumption was collected at the beginning of the study and before anyone was diagnosed with cancer. This particular study design makes the findings more reliable because it reduces the chance that cancer patients remember their beverage consumption differently or report any changes after diagnosis.

Although this is how epidemiologic studies typically determine the relationship between diet and diseases, aspartame estimated this way may or may not reflect lifetime consumption. Also, most diet beverage consum-

> **FAST FACT**
>
> According to the European Food Safety Authority, the recommended maximum acceptable daily intake (ADI) of aspartame is forty milligrams per kilogram of body weight. An average adult would have to drink over thirteen cans of sugar-free drinks every day to reach their maximum ADI for artificial sweeteners.

ers in the study drank moderate amounts of aspartame, ranging from none to 3400 mg daily—and on average 200 mg daily—which is a little over a can of diet soda. While this moderate consumption is reflective of the average consumption in the U.S., these findings limit any conclusions about cancer risk in people who consume very high amounts of aspartame.

Putting the Study into Context

Does the general population drink as much diet soda as the study participants?

The participants of the NIH-AARP Diet and Health Study were recruited from six states and two metropolitan areas around the U.S. that have highly reliable cancer registry data. Thus, the study participants are a good sample of older adults in the U.S. The study questionnaire included questions to identify consumers of diet beverages and aspartame users for coffee and hot tea, which is information rarely available in most large population studies. The average aspartame consumption among diet beverage consumers in the study was about 200 mg per day, which is similar to a survey of U.S. consumers done by the Food and Drug Administration (FDA).

Were there differences in the relationship between aspartame and cancer by racial group, ethnicity, age, or gender?

Researchers examined the relationship between aspartame and lymphoma, leukemia, and malignant brain cancers by different races and age groups and also in men and women separately, and found no difference from the overall finding. However, it should be noted that the study included older adults who were mostly whites.

Do animal studies of aspartame show the same results as human studies?

The NIH-AARP study findings match those of previous animal studies by the FDA and coincide with the conclusion of an earlier study on childhood brain cancers.

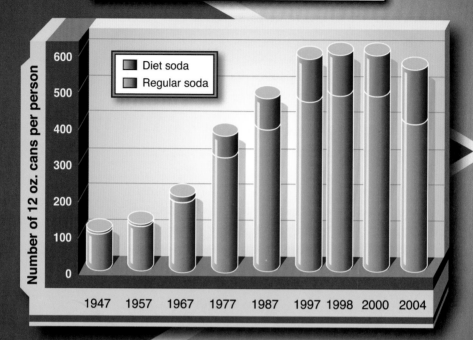

Annual Soft Drink Production in the United States

Number of 12 oz. cans per person

| Diet soda |
| Regular soda |

600
500
400
300
200
100
0

1947 1957 1967 1977 1987 1997 1998 2000 2004

Taken from: USDA Economic Research Service (1947–1987): *Beverage Digest* (1997–2004).

Shortly before this most recent study of aspartame and cancer was published, the European Food Safety Authority reviewed the recent animal data and urged caution when interpreting results. "The increased incidence of lymphomas/leukemias reported in treated rats was unrelated to aspartame, given the high background incidence of chronic inflammatory changes in the lungs and the lack of a positive dose-response relationship."

What are some facts about aspartame?

• Aspartame, distributed under several trade names (e.g., NutraSweet® and Equal®), was approved in 1981 by the FDA after numerous tests showed that it did not cause cancer or other adverse effects in laboratory animals.

- In the NIH-AARP Diet and Health Study, aspartame consumption ranged from 0 to 3400 mg per day (about 19 cans of soda at the high end; however, the upper limit is not absolute because investigators asked multiple-choice questions on frequency and the highest option was "6-plus times a day"). There are 180 mg of aspartame in a 12 ounce can of diet soda.

- The highest aspartame category in the NIH-AARP Diet and Health Study was "600 mg and above per day," or about three or more cans of diet soda; researchers also examined higher categories (more than 1200 mg per day or 2000 mg per day, which is equivalent to approximately seven to 11 cans of soft drinks daily) with fewer people and found similar results of no elevated risk.

- FDA's Acceptable Daily Intake (ADI) of aspartame is 50 mg per kilogram of body weight or about 3,750 mg (21 cans of diet soda) for an adult weighing 75 kilograms (165 lb). ADI is the amount of substance (e.g., food additive) like aspartame that can be consumed daily over a lifetime without appreciable health risk to a person on the basis of all the known facts at the time of the evaluation.

- The average aspartame consumption among diet beverage consumers in the NIH-AARP Diet and Health Study was 200 mg per day, or about 7 percent of the ADI, which is the same as a survey of U.S. consumers done by the FDA.

- An animal study that fed 0, 4, 20, 100, 500, 2500, and 5000 mg per kilogram of body weight of aspartame to rats saw lymphoma/leukemia increase in female rats, starting from about twice the risk with 20 mg per kilogram of body weight (a person weighing 75 kilograms or 165 lbs, consuming 1500 mg aspartame, or about 8 cans of diet soda) compared with a control group that was not fed aspartame.

Findings Are Mixed Concerning a Link Between Electromagnetic Fields and Leukemia

National Cancer Institute, National Institutes of Health

In the following viewpoint the National Cancer Institute reports on research that examines a potential link between exposure to high-voltage power lines, large electric transformers, power substations, and home appliances and an increased risk of childhood leukemia. The authors note that a 1979 study conclusively linked electromagnetic field exposure and leukemia but that more recent studies have produced mixed findings. The National Cancer Institute, part of the U.S. National Institutes of Health, coordinates the National Cancer Program, which conducts, coordinates, and supports cancer education, research, training, and other programs.

*W*hat are electric and magnetic fields?
    Electricity is the movement of electrons, or current, through a wire. The type of electricity that runs through power lines and in houses is alternating current (AC). AC power produces two

SOURCE: "Magnetic Field Exposure and Cancer: Questions and Answers," National Cancer Institute, www.cancer.gov, April 21, 2005.

types of fields (areas of energy)—an electric field and a magnetic field. An electric field is produced by voltage, which is the pressure used to push the electrons through the wire, much like water being pushed through a pipe. As the voltage increases, the electric field increases in strength. A magnetic field results from the flow of current through wires or electrical devices and increases in strength as the current increases. These two fields together are referred to as electric and magnetic fields, or EMFs.

Both electric and magnetic fields are present around appliances and power lines. However, electric fields are easily shielded or weakened by walls and other objects, whereas magnetic fields can pass through buildings, humans, and most other materials. Since magnetic fields are most likely to penetrate the body, they are the component of EMFs that are usually studied in relation to cancer.

The focus of this fact sheet is on extremely low-frequency magnetic fields. Examples of devices that emit these fields include power lines and electrical appliances, such as electric shavers, hair dryers, computers, televisions, electric blankets, and heated waterbeds. Most electrical appliances have to be turned on to produce a magnetic field. The strength of a magnetic field decreases rapidly with increased distance from the source.

When Children Are Exposed to Magnetic Fields

Is there a link between magnetic field exposure at home and cancer in children?

Numerous epidemiological (population) studies and comprehensive reviews have evaluated magnetic field exposure and risk of cancer in children. Since the two most common cancers in children are leukemia and brain tumors, most of the research has focused on these

Beginning in 1979, numerous studies on the effects of electromagnetic fields for a link to leukemia have been mixed. More studies are needed. (© moodboard/ Superstock)

two types. A study in 1979 pointed to a possible association between living near electric power lines and childhood leukemia. Among more recent studies, findings have been mixed. Some have found an association; others have not. These studies are discussed in the following paragraphs. Currently, researchers conclude that there is limited evidence that magnetic fields from power lines cause childhood leukemia, and that there is inadequate evidence that these magnetic fields cause other cancers in children. Researchers have not found a consistent relationship between magnetic fields from power lines or appliances and childhood brain tumors.

In one large study by the National Cancer Institute (NCI) and the Children's Oncology Group, researchers measured magnetic fields directly in homes. This study found that children living in homes with high magnetic field levels did not have an increased risk of childhood acute lymphoblastic leukemia. The one exception may have been children living in homes that had fields greater than 0.4 microtesla (µT), a very high level that occurs in few residences. Another study conducted by NCI researchers reported that children living close to overhead power lines based on distance measurements were not at greater risk of leukemia.

To estimate more accurately the risks of leukemia in children from magnetic fields resulting from power lines, researchers pooled (combined) data from many studies. In one pooled study that combined nine well-conducted studies from several countries, including a study from the NCI, a twofold excess risk of childhood leukemia was associated with exposure to magnetic fields above 0.4 µT. In another pooled study that combined 15 studies, a similar increased risk was seen above 0.3 µT. It is difficult to determine if this level of risk represents a real increase or if it results from study bias. Such study bias can be related to the selection of study subjects or possibly to other factors that relate to levels of magnetic field exposure. If magnetic fields caused childhood leukemia, certain patterns would have been found such as increasing risk with increasing levels of magnetic field exposure.

FAST FACT

Even in studies that link electromagnetic field exposure to leukemia, researchers note that while leukemia risk may have "doubled," the overall risk remains very slight—less than two in ten thousand.

The Use of Everyday Appliances

Another way that people can be exposed to magnetic fields is from household electrical appliances. Several studies have investigated this relationship. Although magnetic fields near many electrical appliances are higher than near power lines, appliances contribute less to a person's total exposure to magnetic fields. This is because most appliances are used only for short periods of time, and most are not used close to the body, whereas power lines are always emitting magnetic fields.

In a detailed evaluation, investigators from NCI and the Children's Oncology Group examined whether the use of household electrical appliances by the mother while pregnant and later by the child increased the risk of childhood leukemia. Although some appliances were associ-

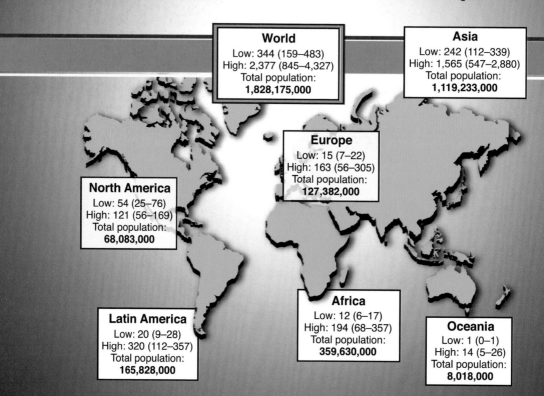

Childhood Leukemia Cases Possibly Linked to Electromagnetic Field Exposure

This map identifies the estimated numbers and ranges of leukemia cases among children younger than fourteen that are possibly attributable to electromagnetic field exposure. The regional ranges are based on the lowest and highest exposure levels from the countries in each of those regions.

World
Low: 344 (159–483)
High: 2,377 (845–4,327)
Total population:
1,828,175,000

Asia
Low: 242 (112–339)
High: 1,565 (547–2,880)
Total population:
1,119,233,000

Europe
Low: 15 (7–22)
High: 163 (56–305)
Total population:
127,382,000

North America
Low: 54 (25–76)
High: 121 (56–169)
Total population:
68,083,000

Latin America
Low: 20 (9–28)
High: 320 (112–357)
Total population:
165,828,000

Africa
Low: 12 (6–17)
High: 194 (68–357)
Total population:
359,630,000

Oceania
Low: 1 (0–1)
High: 14 (5–26)
Total population:
8,018,000

Taken from: Leeka Kheifets, Abdelmonem A. Afifi, and Riti Shimkhada, "Public Health and Impact of Extremely Low-Frequency Electromagnetic Fields," *Environmental Health Perspectives*, October 2006. www.ehponline.org.

ated with childhood leukemia, researchers did not find any consistent pattern of increasing risk with increasing years of use or how often the appliance was used. A few other studies have reported mostly inconsistencies or no relation between appliances and risk of childhood cancer.

Occupational exposure of mothers to high levels of magnetic fields during pregnancy has been associated with childhood leukemia in a Canadian study. Similar studies need to be done in other populations to see if this is indeed the case.

Is there a link between magnetic field exposure in the home and cancer in adults?

Although several studies have looked into the relationship of leukemia, brain tumors, and breast cancer in adults exposed to magnetic fields in the home, there are only a few large studies with long-term, magnetic field measurements. No consistent association between magnetic fields and leukemia or brain tumors has been established.

The majority of epidemiological studies have shown no relationship between breast cancer in women and magnetic fields from electrical appliances. Recent studies of breast cancer and magnetic fields in the home have included direct and indirect magnetic field measurements. These studies mostly found no association between breast cancer in females and magnetic fields from power lines or electric blankets. A Norwegian study found a risk for exposure to magnetic fields in the home, and a study in African-American women found that use of electric bedding devices may increase breast cancer risk.

When Workers Are Near Power Sources Every Day

Is there a link between magnetic field exposure at work and cancer in adults?

Several studies conducted in the 1980s and early 1990s reported that people who worked in some electrical occupations (such as power station operators and phone line workers) had higher than expected rates of some types of cancer, particularly leukemia, brain tumors, and male breast cancer. Some occupational studies showed very small increases in risk for leukemia and brain cancer, but these results were based on job titles and not actual measurements. More recently conducted studies that have included both job titles and individual exposure measurements have no consistent finding of an increasing risk of leukemia, brain tumors, or female breast cancer with increasing exposure to magnetic fields at work.

What have scientists learned from animal experiments about the relationship between magnetic field exposure and cancer?

Animal studies have not found that magnetic field exposure is associated with increased risk of cancer. The absence of animal data supporting carcinogenicity makes it biologically less likely that magnetic field exposures in humans, at home or at work, are linked to increased cancer risk.

CHAPTER 3

Patients, Families, and Survivors Cope with Leukemia

Caring for a Child with Leukemia

Gordon Livingston

In the following selection Gordon Livingston recounts his family's experiences after his son Lucas received a bone marrow transplant in order to restore and repopulate his healthy blood cells. Livingston was the donor, and Lucas suffered major complications when his father's functional immune cells attacked his unfamiliar body. Lucas died in 1992, just weeks after his bone marrow transplant. He was six years old. Gordon Livingston is a psychiatrist and the author of three books.

March 30, 1992. Three days after the transplant now with no complications evident, for Lucas at least. Both [my daughter]Nina and I have developed fevers, with headaches and lethargy. My temperature tonight went to 102.3, so I can't even visit the hospital for fear of giving my infection to Lucas. Each day without complications seems a miracle and our spirits

SOURCE: Gordon Livingston, *Only Spring.* New York, NY: HarperSanFrancisco, 1995. Copyright © 1995 by Gordon Livingston, M.D. Reprinted with permission of the Carol Mann Agency.

rise. His blood counts are dropping dramatically; fever and mouth sores are supposed to be next. We are daring to hope that he will surprise everyone and get through this easily. The first seven to fourteen days after the transplant are supposed to be the time for the first signs of GVHD graft-versus-host-disease. He remains energetic: he rides his Big Wheel around the ward for exercise and [my wife] Clare and [my daughter] Emily have stayed healthy to sustain him. I can't imagine why I continue to have a fever. Maybe I can have all the complications for him. I imagine my marrow taking root at the center of his being and beginning to manufacture the cells that will be his new immune system. His counts apparently don't begin rising until week three, so there may be rough spots ahead. Good wishes from others, known and unknown, continue to pour in. His room is a remarkable, healing place with dozens of pictures of well-wishers covering an entire wall.

I think that now I may be ready to grow old without the fear and regret that I always anticipated. My gift to Lucas, if successful, will give me a permanent sense of accomplishment, one that exceeds anything else I might have done or could ever do. . . .

April 5, 1992. Friday brought what I hope is the low point for us. Lucas looked terrible: puffy, feverish with temperatures regularly over 104, delirious much of the time, a rash covering his whole body. The first reading by the doctors was that this indicated GVHD. He was so out of it I was afraid he was dying and, while the nurse changed his bed, I just held him in my arms on the cot in his room and wept. Then the fever remitted and he looks a lot better. The rash also started to appear more drug-related to the staff and they seemed to relax, so our good spirits returned. Clare maintained her equanimity, at least outwardly, though Emily was more like me: terrified. By the end of the day the crisis had passed. It was the burning feel of his skin and the sense of him having no immune system to protect him from infection that brought me to the edge of panic. I spent that night at the hospital, sleeping in a chair. Yesterday he had a lot of diarrhea, but his temperature stayed down and he was a bit more alert. When his mind drifts, it does so in the sweetest, six-year-old way. He says things like "lollipops" and "Miss Piggy," and sometimes breaks into a little smile when asleep. Emily was talking to him while "Wheel of Fortune" was on the TV and, after one puzzle, he said softly, as he often does at home, "Dad got it." Sometimes, when awake, he bursts into tears and says, "I want to go home!" When we explain the need to be in the hospital a while longer, he asks, "Can I go home just to visit?"

This morning Clare called to say that his diarrhea stopped about 1:00 A.M. *and* that his white blood cell count this morning was 134! This is far below normal but is the first indication that my marrow has taken and is starting to function. At a white blood count of 1000 they begin to think of discharge, so we are on our way....

April 19, 1992. (Day twenty-three.) Easter. The last ten nights I've stayed at the hospital with Clare to help with Lucas's intractable diarrhea. It has been an agonizing time with incredible ups and downs: fevers, blood pressure drops, rapid heartbeat, irregular breathing; times when he looked so sick I thought he might die in front of us. The rashes have been variable, and the inevitable drug side effects have made him look swollen and puffy. He has come to resemble his birth picture: no hair, face so swollen he looks like he's been beaten up. Through it all he has remained uncomplaining, only occasionally asking to go home. His white blood cell count has come up to 2,200 and they don't think he has an infection. Another skin biopsy from his back showed "mild GVHD" to go along with the graft versus host problem in his bowel. We anxiously watch his diarrhea volume. He is now at maximal levels of immunosuppressants and getting a course of seven treatments with "anti-thymocytic globulin," derived from, of all things, horse serum.

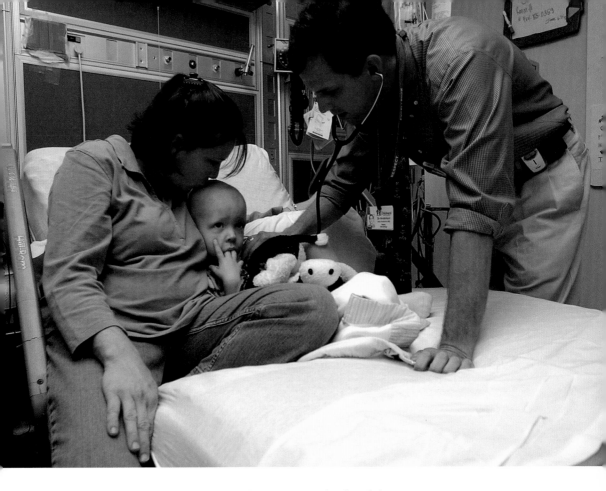

A three-year-old leukemia patient is examined while his mother provides support. (**AP Photo/John Bazemore**)

I thought I had been through some tough, fearful moments in my life, but they are as nothing compared with the horror of these nights. There are some losses that simply can't be contemplated. One encouraging moment came on a night when he was feverish and practically unconscious. One of the nurses, sensing our distress, looked at him and said, "He's just lying there healing." Over the last few days he has seemed clinically better, more alert and engaged, watching some TV. He's been able to do a couple of laps around the ward even though it's hard for him. I see him as recovering, however slowly; I just wish the diarrhea would stop. When it does, he should be ready for discharge. What a thought! Lucas at home, playing in his room, sleeping in our bed. *On this, the celebration of Christ's return from the dead, I ask you, O Lord, to give us back our son.*

The day before yesterday I was giving platelets for him to use, a two-hour procedure. Lying on the bed, a needle in each arm, I looked at the clock and noticed that it was three minutes past noon on Good Friday.

April 21, 1992. (Day twenty-five.) How I long for the prosaic concerns of everyday life. I am just beginning to understand the meaning of chronic anxiety. The emotional ups and downs occasioned by the daily variations in Lucas's symptoms are a roller coaster in which we imagine we see an improving trend, as we must, since the alternative is too awful to contemplate. His liver functions are abnormal and it is hard not to panic. His diarrhea was down in volume yesterday but rose again today. Nightly, he spikes a fever that leads to blood cultures, chest films, and so on. Through it all Clare is better able to maintain her composure than I, in spite of the fact that she has been at the hospital continuously now for thirty-four days. I've spent the last ten to twelve nights there, but came home tonight to be with Emily and take her to school tomorrow. Today Lucas talked a lot about the places he wants to go when he gets out: Rehoboth Beach, Squam Lake, the Bahamas, a cruise, even "a hotel." How soon will it be before I can look at my son without an imminent fear for his life? Even the prospect of daily outpatient visits for one hundred days, or a surgical mask in public for six months, or a year away from school seems as nothing compared with this day-to-day oscillation between optimism and unspeakable dread.

April 23, 1992. (Day twenty-seven.) The news is mixed. A biopsy of the lower bowel yesterday was equivocal but indicated the probability of continuing GVHD. His skin looks worse and itches a lot. His diarrhea has definitely decreased, good news.

We are beginning to understand this battle against GVHD as a sort of holding action: using the immunosuppressants to keep it in check until it "burns itself out" while hoping not to be overwhelmed by "complications" (infection, liver disease) in the meantime. Rick Jones, the attending oncologist now, seems guarded in his attitude, and it is hard to sustain our determined optimism in the face of Lucas's recurrent high fevers and general lassitude and discomfort. Just when I feel the most scared, however, he rallies and starts taking an interest in things like TV cartoons or begins to talk about what he wants to do when he gets out—go back to school, play with his friends. He is on fluid restriction which, naturally, causes him to ask repeatedly for water.

Sustaining Emily's morale is another issue. When Lucas is feverish or uncomfortable late in the day, I can't bear to spend the night away from him, so I end up taking Emily to stay at a friend's house. I know she longs to spend time with her mom, but Lucas's need for Clare's constant presence holds her captive. God, I wish this nightmare were past and we could all be healthy and together in one of the places that we love.

April 26, 1992. (Day thirty.) Today marks the low point—so far. On rounds this morning Rick Jones looked at Lucas's rash, which now covers about 90 percent of his body, and asked Clare and me to step outside. He wanted us to know that he viewed the rash as likely GVHD and regarded as "an unfavorable sign" the fact that it had gotten worse in the face of the immunosuppressants. He also said, "We've used all the guns in our arsenal." His statements sounded tinged with hopelessness and I found myself sweating and nauseated, near to collapse. We gathered ourselves quickly and reassured each other about the uncertainty of diagnosing a rash and the need to give him time to heal.

They are increasing the steroids dramatically for three days in what seems a desperate attempt to control the GVHD. They are also adding an antibiotic to combat a positive blood culture. Lucas continues to be swollen with fluid. His diarrhea mercifully is less.

He was alert this morning and I lay with him and watched *The Ewok Adventure* on the Disney Channel. He may look worse to the doctors, but his spirit and ability to interact and look to the future give us all a lift. He again said that he wanted to visit Squam Lake. I wonder if a merciful God will grant us this modest but miraculous indulgence.

This dance with death, this forced contemplation of the unimaginable is wearing but endurable in the context of being able to be with Lucas, to love him and feel his love in return. There is pain in the unfairness of his having to go through this, but pleasure, privilege really, in helping him. My world has shrunk to the size of this hospital room; everything else exists somewhere in the realm of events that have nothing to do with me.

Nine hours later and our spirits are much improved. Lucas had a good day, itchy but alert. On the phone to his aunt Julie on her birthday, he even laughed a couple of times. His rash seems to be improving from the neck down, which the nurse says is characteristic of GVHD. He has no fever and the new antibiotic may have gotten to that infection in his blood. It definitely felt like a healing day. This is not, repeat not, a dying child. The increase in the [steroid] prednisone may be helping, of course, but I just see him getting better, talking about vacations, fishing, his aunt Julie "eating popcorn off the floor." . . . *Thank you God, for this day. Please give us more like it.*

May 4, 1992. Tonight I feel close to despair. Lucas's face is swollen again, his eyes almost closed, his lips and ears crusted. More ominous, his legs are sloughing skin. His feet look blackened and gangrenous. He is also jaundiced and his lab studies show liver damage. The high-dose immunosuppressants are toxic to his kidneys. The doctors seem surprised that he is not leaking fluid into his lungs, though that will inevitably occur if the GVHD progresses. He is intruded upon constantly: by physical

FAST FACT

Leukemia is the most common cancer in children and teens, accounting for about 33 percent of all childhood cancers. Acute lymphocytic leukemia is the most common form of childhood leukemia.

therapy, ophthalmology, bathing, ointment applications, weighing, vital signs, blood drawing. Through it all, he remains stoic and uncomplaining. It is impossible to give up hope when he remains so responsive, interested in tapes and TV, loving and brave. Clare is indomitably optimistic and I must be also. Emily is scared but tries not to show it or perhaps even admit it to herself. We all soldier on in the hope that catastrophe will not overtake him before this dreadful disease burns out. . . .

May 5, 1992. (Day thirty-nine.) Another "corridor conference" called this morning by Rick Jones to verify that, if the worst happens and Lucas is overtaken by a lung infection, we will support their "aggressive" care plan of intubation and transfer to the Pediatric Intensive Care Unit. He said that he didn't anticipate this occurring, but at this high level of immunosuppressants, infection remains a dangerous threat. Rick characterized the treatment now as "a race" between complications and a remission in the GVHD. It's astonishing how much uncertainty we have come to tolerate. During a quiet moment this morning, I thought of the ego-obliterating aspects of this whole experience. Nothing in my life has been as important or as hard for me to influence as this struggle for Lucas's life. Just being here to help catch his urine, give him water, carry him to and from his bath, hold him while he's weighed is very little and more than enough. The whole meaning of this illness, indeed his entire life, has been to love him as much as we can for as long as we can. It is at once my obligation and deepest pleasure. Nothing else matters, so this is what we do. . . .

May 7, 1992. Lucas continues to have morning fever spikes. What is it? Infection? GVHD? No one is sure. He craves milk, which we ration to prevent diarrhea. He talks about pizza, the mall, watches cartoon tapes and the Disney Channel. It's so hard to remember us there at Disney World with Lucas healthy and running around, meeting his hero Mickey Mouse. It feels like we have been in this hospital forever; one day runs into the next, but toward what end?

As Lucas has gotten more swollen and unwieldy, the twice-daily weighing ceremony has become increasingly important to me, and I think to him. When the nurse's aide brings the scale in the room, he looks at me and reaches out his arm to place it around my neck. I slide my arms carefully under his knees and shoulders, lift him, and step onto the scale. This is not a comfortable process for him with his tender skin, but he endures it uncomplainingly. We hope each time for a decrease toward his "ideal weight," and each tenth of a kilo in that direction is cause for rejoicing in the same way that every normal temperature is welcomed. As Clare and I changed his diaper tonight, he looked at me and said, "I love your voice, I love your face."

May 8, 1992. (Day forty-two.) Lucas's liver studies look worse. A sonogram is going to be done today to rule out gallstones, but if this is negative there appears to be nothing to do but watch and wait. His speech has become slurred, his breathing labored. He has a fever with chills and is very jaundiced. Is this the end? *Please, God, no.*

My mother, I have recently learned, suffers from Alzheimer's disease. This fate may be in my genes too, and I might at some point have to face the loss of my past. Perhaps by the time this happens I will welcome it. Some memories are too terrible for the heart to hold.

A Father Grieves for His Adult Son

Gary Cartwright

In the following selection Gary Cartwright writes about a final journey, a road trip, with his adult son Mark who was suffering from leukemia. Cartwright and his son set out to find new leaves from a desert plant rumored by Native American and New Age herbalists to have healing properties. He acknowledges that the search for the ingredients of a healing tea was a last—and desperate—grasp at finding a cure for Mark's illness. Cartwright discusses how their last trip together paralleled his own emotional preparation for his son's death—especially with the help of his son's optimism and grace. Gary Cartwright is a staff writer and featured contributor at Texas Monthly *as well as the author of several books.*

I was flying blind. Nothing in my experience gave me a frame of reference for this journey. My son Mark was dying of acute leukemia, and the two of us were racing across the margins of the Chihuahuan Desert east of Van Horn [Texas], searching for the new top leaves

SOURCE: Gary Cartwright, "Nothing to It," *Texas Monthly,* vol. 25, June 1997, pp. 78–81, 113–114. Copyright 1997 Texas Monthly, Inc. Reproduced by permission.

of the creosote bush, which when brewed into a tea were considered a cure for the disease by some Mexican curanderos [medicine men]. I had learned this in a letter from a man who was doing twenty years on a drug charge in federal prison. I have received hundreds of letters from people in prison, but they always wanted something from me. This guy just wanted to do me a favor. Mark and I both knew that it was the longest of long shots, but long shots were all we had.

The trip was in early March [1997], about six weeks before Mark died. It was long and arduous, and it sapped what little strength he had left. The letter had explained that the two of us had to leave a "gift of water" for the creosote plants. We flew from Austin to Dallas to Midland, then drove 125 miles to an isolated place within sight of

For the parents of children who suffer from leukemia, the one unanswerable question is, "Why did my child contract this disease?" (AFP/Getty Images)

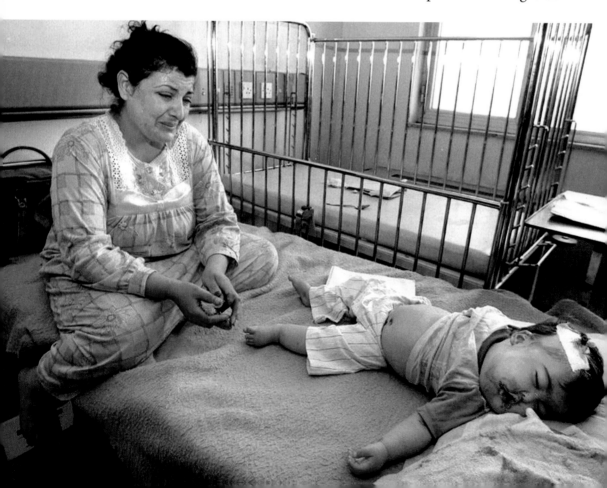

the Davis Mountains, two liter bottles of Evian in the seat between us. Mark slept almost all the way, racked with fever, chills, and nausea. After collecting three bags of leaves, we spent the night in a Midland motel, the kid so sick that I wondered if he'd make it through the night. I was awake until two in the morning, talking long distance to friends and family, trying to figure out our next move.

Mark's condition was diagnosed in July 1996 at a cancer clinic in Atlanta, Georgia, the city where he grew up after his mother and I divorced and where he had lived since his own divorce in early '94. He had undergone six intensive doses of chemotherapy, whose powerful toxins destroy cancer cells—and good cells as well. I suspect that one day we'll look back at this wretched procedure the way we look back with revulsion at frontal lobotomies. But chemotherapy was the only treatment available for Mark's type of leukemia. It wouldn't cure him, but it could possibly put the cancer into remission long enough for doctors to perform a bone marrow transplant.

Looking for a Matching Bone Marrow Donor

We had searched without success for a bone marrow donor for nine months. Unfortunately, no one in our family was a match, and neither were any of the 2.7 million people on the National Bone Marrow Registry. Among Caucasians, a match exists for a given patient about 80 percent of the time; among minorities, the figure drops to about 50 percent. One doctor speculated that finding a match for Mark was so difficult because there are traces of Native American blood in our family, but he was just guessing. Anecdotal evidence suggests that genetic tissue typing for bone marrow produces unexpected results. In 1993 Anne Connally, the daughter-in-law of John Connally, turned out to be the world's only perfect match for a sixteen-year-old Japanese girl, who is alive and doing well today because Mrs. Connally was tested and added to the national registry in 1990.

In January and February [1997], Mark's family and friends had staged testing drives in Atlanta, Little Rock, and Austin, adding another 1,500 people to the national registry, yet still there was no perfect match. We were desperate. Even [as] we slept, even as we prayed, the clock was ticking. After my wife, Phyllis, and I ran a full-page ad in *Texas Monthly*, pleading for help, people called from all over the country, volunteering to be tested, extending their support, and contributing money to the Leukemia Society of America. Rosalind Wright, a sister of Austin writer Lawrence Wright, telephoned from Lexington, Massachusetts, where she had rallied thirteen tribes of Native Americans and personnel from a military base to get tested. A friend in California who is a Buddhist monk sent a seed blessed by the Dalai Lama with instructions on how Mark was to ingest it. The pilgrimage to the desert was only one in a series of things we tried.

The worst day of my life—worse even than the day Mark died—started early the next morning, when I drove Mark to Midland International Airport for a flight back to Atlanta. Until then I hadn't realized how far the disease had progressed. He was so weak that I doubt he could have walked unassisted to the gate. I helped him into a wheelchair and pushed him. He had eaten almost nothing for a week, so we stopped at the coffee bar; I bought him a Coke and a banana, and he was able to keep them down. For two days he had said almost nothing. A question that needed a response got a nod or a shake of the head. Looking at him then, as pale and weak as a newborn puppy, I couldn't help but remember that a year before, Mark and I had worked out together at my gym in Austin, both of us fit and seemingly invincible. As recently as Christmas 1996 he had looked reasonably strong and cheerful. But now you could almost see his life leaking away.

When it was time for him to board the plane, we hugged and kissed, knowing it might be our final goodbye. I was close to tears. Watching my son shuffle slowly down the ramp to his plane, his hairless head bowed in agony, his clothes hanging off his emaciated frame, a kid who had just turned forty but looked ninety, I kept thinking, Why him? Why not me? When a child dies, "Why?" is the last question to go away. . . .

Adult Leukemia Progresses Differently from Childhood Leukemia

In Greek, "Leukemia" means "white blood." Mark had M-5 leukemia, the most severe type of adult acute myelogenous leukemia, in which immature white blood cells called blasts take over the bone marrow and prevent it from making enough normal white and red cells and platelets. The blasts overwhelm the mature white cells that fight infection, the red cells that carry oxygen, and the platelets that help blood clot, spilling into the bloodstream and infiltrating organs and glands until the process of life shuts down. M-5 is particularly nasty and extremely resistant to chemotherapy.

Scientists don't know what causes leukemia, only that there are different types that react differently to treatment: Children's leukemia can be cured, for instance, while adult leukemia is almost always fatal. Victims of chronic leukemia sometimes live for years because the blasts are more mature and progress more slowly, but eventually the production of immature white cells quickens, and chronic leukemia progresses into acute leukemia.

Aubrey Thompson, a friend at the University of Texas Medical Branch at Galveston who has done leukemia research for twenty years, told me that Mark may have had chronic leukemia for the past ten or even twenty years, even though no one had detected it. "What makes adult leukemia so extremely difficult is that the cancer cells come and go, hiding out most of the time," he said. "You go along for years, having a few bad days when you feel tired or run-down or flulike; then one day it explodes into acute leukemia. In childhood leukemia, by contrast, the cancer cells are very active. They come out of hiding and grow rapidly, and therefore they are sensitive to certain drugs and can be wiped out."

A bone marrow transplant is the only complete cure for leukemia known at this time, but the process is long and dangerous, littered with formidable obstacles and treacherous ifs (if chemotherapy can force the cancer into temporary remission . . .). The transplant procedure is enormously expensive—it can cost up to $250,000—and it's highly risky: Between 40 and 60 percent of those who undergo a transplant survive, and some survivors of the bone marrow transplant later succumb to fatal complications from graft-versus-host disease.

Of course, to have a transplant you must have a matching donor, another treacherous if: One in four leukemia patients who need a transplant never find a donor. Part of the problem is that most people have never heard of the National Marrow Donor Program. Among all diseases, leukemia is the number one killer of children—and it afflicts ten times as many adults as children—yet it is not high-profile. In a nation of more than 267 million people, fewer than 3 million are on the [donor] registry and fewer than 600,000 are minorities. Another problem is money. Because genetic tissue typing is so expensive, most people who are tested are asked to pay a fee, usually between $45 and $75 (since there are so few minorities on the registry, their tests are free). The cost aside, however, getting tested is really pretty easy. It takes only a couple of minutes: You fill out a short medical history and let a technician draw two small blood samples, which are sent to a national laboratory to be analyzed for the antigens needed to make a match. The identity codes of the antigens are then recorded in the national registry's computer. If your antigens match a leukemia patient's, you'll be called in for more tests. Six out of six matching antigens are a "miracle match."

At any point, of course, a potential donor can back out. Shirley Laine, the bone marrow manager of the Central Texas Regional Blood and Tissue Center in Austin, told me the heartbreaking story of Victor Ojeda, a nine-year-old Austin boy who died after a woman who was a perfect match decided she didn't want to go through the ordeal of a transplant. It's not really that much of an ordeal, though. As a donor, you spend a day or two in a hospital, during which time a needle is injected into your hip and marrow is extracted from the upper back part of the pelvis. You'll have a sore butt for a week or two, but that's a small price for saving a life. . .

Mark Chooses to Go Home

I know now that even if we had found a miracle match for Mark, a transplant would have been useless. All that horrible chemotherapy had destroyed his immune system and had done great damage to his organs, but it never came close to stopping the cancer or putting it into remission. Mark's doctor, Daniel Dubovsky, compared cancer cells to cockroaches: "You might kill ninety-five percent of them," he told us, "but the remaining five percent emerge stronger and more resistant." Dubovsky encounters only one or two patients a year whose cancer is so virulent that it resists the strongest chemotherapy. Mark happened to be one. "He lived nine or ten months longer than a lot of people who do go into remission," Dubovsky said. "He had magnificent strength and energy."

Two and a half weeks after our journey to the Chihuahuan Desert, while Mark was in the hospital, Dubovsky informed him that there was nothing left he could do. We were devastated. Markie said he'd like to go home.

Phyllis and I flew to Atlanta for the deathwatch, not sure how we would handle it but trusting that Markie would set the style. Getting reacquainted with his long-time group of pals, we realized he'd set the style years ago. In high school he had put together a combination rock band and chili cookoff team called the Chain Gang, and they were with him until the end, honoring his wish that nobody feel sorry for him or for themselves. Tom "Meat" Smith, Markie's oldest friend, sat at the foot of his bed and regaled us with stories about the Great Cartwright. It seems that the women of Atlanta were not quite unanimous in their devotion. Meat told us about one woman Mark jilted when he worked for the Turner Broadcasting System. To this day, she is unable to speak his name without pausing to spit on the floor. Meat demonstrated, feigning a high-pitched voice: "Oh, you must be referring to Mark . . . hock, spitooowee . . . Cartwright." Sick as he was, Mark doubled over with laughter.

Also on hand was the latest and last of Mark's girlfriends, Susan Shaw. She was as tough and as tenacious as they come. Almost single-handedly she had organized a drive that put five hundred new names on the bone marrow registry. She could have bailed out at any time—no one would have blamed her—but Susan wasn't the type to bail. The only time she lost it was the day Dubovsky told the family it was over. "It wasn't supposed to be that way," Susan said later, her eyes swollen and red from a day of crying. "I had imagined our twilight years, sitting on the porch watching our grandchildren. Suddenly I just went to pieces. I was crying and calling out to God, saying, 'Why Mark? Why me?'" Soon after, Susan got a phone call from the National Marrow Donor Program, telling her that she was a partial match for a 54-year-old man in the Midwest. "God works in mysterious ways," she concluded.

Visiting Mark for the Last Time

What got us through those last few weeks was Markie's remarkable courage, the grace, dignity, and measured good humor with which he faced death. He had resolved to put his affairs in order, and that's what he did. He dictated a will and made it known that when the end came he didn't want the paramedics to resuscitate him. He asked that his body be cremated and his ashes scattered in the Gulf of Mexico. (One exception: Some of the ashes would be handed over to the Chain Gang, whose members would select an appropriate urn—most likely a cowboy boot—and take them each year to the chili cookoff in Athens, Georgia.) He selected a Cajun friend, Jonathan "Gator" Ordoyne, as his replacement in the Chain Gang.

I asked him if he was scared. "No," he said, "strangely enough I'm not." He had been sick for so long that what he really wanted was just "a few good days." That became my prayer: "If you can't give us the miracle of sparing his life, Lord, then grant our fallback position: a few good days, then let him die quickly and without pain or fear."

My prayer was answered. Markie seemed to get better by the day. He got out of bed and spent several hours sitting in the sun. He was able to eat solid food and even hold down cups of the creosote tea. He went to a couple of movies with Susan, and the three of us spent an afternoon at the Atlanta Botanical Garden. We drove the rural back roads, where spectacular explosions of azaleas, redbuds, and dogwoods seemed to have blossomed specifically on Mark's behalf, and had dinner at his favorite Mexican restaurant.

The time had come for me to go home, we both agreed. "You've got to go sometime," Markie said, not unaware of the double meaning. My last night in Atlanta we had dinner at his favorite Thai restaurant, then Mark and Susan drove me back to my hotel. Standing there face to face in the parking lot was the hardest part. Neither of us wanted to drag it out. Mark kissed me and said he loved me. I said I loved him too. "I can't bring myself to say good-bye," I told him. "So, until I see you again."

> **FAST FACT**
>
> Leukemia causes an estimated twenty-two thousand deaths in the United States each year.

"Until I see you again," he told me back. I turned toward the hotel entrance, knowing it wouldn't be in this lifetime.

Coping with Losing a Loved One

After that we talked daily by phone. Mark told me that he and Meat were driving to Augusta for the opening day of the Masters golf tournament. On Friday, April 11, he flew to Little Rock to visit his children, nine-year-old Katy and seven-year-old Malcolm. It was an act of sheer will. His fever had returned, signaling that the brief reprieve was over. He somehow made it back to Atlanta on Sunday afternoon and died early the next morning. His last words were to Susan. "I think this is it," he said softly, closing his eyes. "I'm packing 'em in."

Dealing with the "why" question is the ultimate test of faith. It took me a while to realize that God is not there to answer "Why" questions, though He can help ease the other emotions that overtake a parent whose child dies: the guilt, the frustration, the anger. What should I have done? What could I have done? Phyllis told me that when her son Robert was dying of AIDS in 1994, she had an irresistible urge to hold him tightly, as though she might transfer her energy and her wellness to him. I felt the same urge.

Anger was the emotion that hit hardest and lasted longest. I was angry at his doctor and at the hospital for allowing him to waste away; there must have been something else they could have done. I hated the entire pharmaceutical industry for wallowing in profits while its researchers consistently failed to find cures. I even called my pal Aubrey Thompson to vent my anger. He assured me that research was doing the best it could.

I no longer waste time on guilt or anger. I miss Markie and think about him almost constantly—not the way he was at the end but the way I knew him for forty years. He hated negative energy. He wouldn't have had it any other way.

A Young Girl's Fight Against Acute Lymphocytic Leukemia

Fred Hutchinson Cancer Research Center

Alyson Looney was diagnosed with acute lymphocytic leukemia (ALL) when she was eight months old. Alyson's parents were told that their infant had a particularly aggressive form of ALL. However, after chemotherapy and a bone marrow transplant, Alyson survived and was in remission by her second birthday. At age four Alyson was still coping with some side effects from her leukemia treatment, but her parents and physicians remained confident that these symptoms would subside over time. The Fred Hutchinson Cancer Research Center was established in 1975 and helped pioneer bone marrow transplants for the treatment of leukemia.

Captured between the covers of a thick blue binder, the memories of Alyson Looney's fight against acute lymphocytic leukemia echo in the copies of e-mails sent by her mother to family and friends.

The e-mails tell the story of an infant whose cell count was off the charts and who had a 25 percent chance of survival

SOURCE: "Alyson Looney," Fred Hutchinson Cancer Research Center, fhcrc.org, 2003. Reproduced by permission.

before the treatment she received by Fred Hutchinson Cancer Research Center physicians at the Seattle Cancer Care Alliance—including a bone-marrow transplant when she was just 14 months old—saved her life.

Seated at the kitchen table in her home near Mill Creek, Wash., Leanne Looney turned the pages of the blue binder as she recounted her daughter's diagnosis, treatment and recovery. "Someday, when Alyson is old enough to understand, I will be able to share these e-mails with her and explain her cancer story," said Leanne.

Just then, Alyson arrived at the table clutching a long-haired doll. "Here comes Rapunzel. Here comes Rapunzel," she said as she slowly marched the doll across the table top.

Leanne, by now accustomed to her 4-year-old daughter's incurable exuberance, smiled and shook her head. "With all that Alyson has experienced at such a young age—chemotherapy, radiation and a bone-marrow transplant, not to mention all the doctor appointments—I expected Alyson to be a shy or withdrawn little girl, but she's just the opposite," she said. "She's friendly, outgoing and loves to be the center of attention. Alyson enjoys seeing her doctors and loves the attention she receives from them!"

Leanne and her husband, Andy, a landscape architect, had been married four years when Alyson, their first child, was born on Aug. 27, 1999. "I had a very normal and healthy pregnancy," said Leanne.

Alyson Is Diagnosed with Leukemia

Their first clue that something might be amiss came when Alyson was 8 months old and sustained a bruise on her forehead that wouldn't go away. Then Alyson grew lethargic and didn't want to eat or drink. Even so, leukemia "never came to mind," said Leanne.

In early May 2000, the Looneys learned the terrible truth. After making a doctor's appointment for Alyson later in the week, Andy discovered a hard mass in Alyson's abdomen. The next day was a Saturday, but rather than wait for Alyson's midweek appointment, Andy took her to the doctor while Leanne went to work at her sales job at a downtown hotel.

Presented with the list of Alyson's symptoms—persistent bruises, lethargy, the abdominal mass—the doctor immediately told Andy to take Alyson to Children's Hospital and Regional Medical Center in Seattle for further tests and diagnoses. "Andy knew right then something was wrong," said Leanne.

Andy called Leanne en route to Children's explaining what had happened. When Andy and Alyson arrived at the emergency room at Children's, blood tests, x-rays and an ultrasound were performed. An hour later, Andy called again and told Leanne to come to the hospital right away. "We still didn't know exactly what was wrong, but my mind was just racing," she recalled. "How could something be wrong with our daughter?"

About three hours after Leanne arrived, four doctors entered the waiting room. "We knew it was bad news," said Leanne. "It doesn't take four doctors to deliver good news."

"The short answer," said one of the doctors, "is that your daughter has leukemia."

"Once I heard that," said Leanne, "I didn't hear the rest of the conversation. Questions started racing through my mind. Why is this happening to us? Have we been bad parents? Is it my fault she has cancer?

"Andy and I were in a state of shock," she said. "Just a few hours before we were a happy normal family getting ready to enjoy a typical Saturday. We thought Alyson probably had some virus. Now we were faced with a parent's worst nightmare—our child has cancer."

Alyson Begins Treatment

Any degree of cancer would have been devastating news, but the extent of Alyson's illness shocked even her doctors.

Acute lymphocytic leukemia (ALL), the most common childhood leukemia, causes the body to produce a dangerously high count of immature white blood cells known as lymphocytes. A healthy person's lymphocyte count ranges between 5–12,000. ALL patients are typically diagnosed with counts of 50–100,000. Alyson was diagnosed with a count of 1.6 million.

> **FAST FACT**
>
> From 1996 to 2003, the five-year survival rate for children under five diagnosed with acute lymphocytic leukemia rose to over 90 percent.

"The doctors said they'd never heard of anyone having that high of a count," said Leanne. "They were surprised that even with a count like that, she was still functioning and still smiling. You wouldn't have known she was sick other than her being lethargic and a little pale. That's what made her diagnosis so hard to believe. She looked pretty healthy, but was so sick on paper!"

Placed immediately in the intensive care unit at Children's, Alyson was given a 25 percent chance of survival, said Leanne. After three days of treatment, however, the family got encouraging news. Medications and a technique called apheresis, which filtered excess lymphocytes out of Alyson's blood, had knocked Alyson's count down to 6,400. Doctors were amazed that Alyson didn't experience kidney failure or any other complications.

Still, Alyson would require numerous rounds of chemotherapy to drive her leukemia into remission. She was transferred to the oncology unit, where she spent the next six weeks. Throughout Alyson's hospitalization, Leanne remained at her daughter's side, eating, sleeping and showering at the hospital. "I got to know all the nurses and doctors by name," she said. "They became like family to us. We even spent our very first Mother's Day together in the hospital. As long as I could be with Alyson, it didn't matter where we were."

When the Looneys first learned Alyson had leukemia, they were prepared to move "wherever we needed to go to get the best care for her," said Leanne. "But we were told we already were at the best place."

Children's is one of three partners of the Seattle Cancer Care Alliance (SCCA). Through the SCCA, the cancer-care resources of Fred Hutchinson, UW Medicine and Children's Hospital and Regional Medical Center are combined to make it one of the most comprehensive cancer-care organizations in the nation.

Alyson left the hospital just in time to spend Father's Day at home. Although she returned regularly to the hospital for more chemotherapy and for a while had to be fed intravenously, she was in remission. Two months shy of her first birthday, Alyson had fought cancer and won.

A Clinical Trial Bone Marrow Transplant

Even so, doctors told the Looneys that chemotherapy alone was unlikely to produce a permanent cure. For that, Alyson, who had a high-risk form of ALL, would need a bone-marrow transplant. "We were told that only one out of 17 children treated with chemotherapy alone survived," said Leanne. "Doctors encouraged us to participate in a clinical trial involving bone-marrow transplants that was being conducted by Fred Hutchinson doctors."

The Looneys decided to pursue the transplant as soon as possible. "If we opted not to do the transplant, then we faced the risk of a relapse and undergoing more chemotherapy, making it even harder to get into remission again," explained Leanne. "Plus we knew the clinical trial would benefit cancer research."

Ideally, Andy, Leanne or another relative would have been Alyson's donor, but their tissue types did not match, so the Looneys turned to the National Marrow Donor Program registry to find an unrelated donor. While a search of the registry failed to find a perfect match, it did turn up a viable one. At first, the Looneys agonized over whether they should wait for a perfect donor, but with no guarantee one would ever be found, they opted to proceed.

The hardest part for Leanne was watching Alyson endure the high-dose chemotherapy and total-body radiation required to kill her old marrow in preparation for the transplant. "I was just a wreck!" she said. "It was so heartbreaking exposing my little girl to such high doses of chemotherapy and radiation, knowing that I am actually killing a part of her. There was no turning back and there were no guarantees that this transplant was going to work.

"I just prayed and prayed that everything was going to work out and that someday this could all be put behind us," said Leanne. "Alyson's laughter, positive attitude and continuous smiles all through the transplant gave me the strength and courage I needed in order to care for her."

It was at the Fred Hutchinson Cancer Research Institute in Seattle, Wahington, that Alyson Looney received treatment and a bone marrow transplant that saved her life. (AFP/Getty Images)

Alyson received her transplant on Oct. 25, 2000. She spent 38 days in the hospital before the family moved into an apartment in the Pete Gross House in order to be close to the SCCA clinic while Alyson recovered and received follow-up care. They returned home Feb. 1, 2001.

One year after transplant, the Looneys learned the name of Alyson's bone-marrow donor. Although they haven't met the donor yet—she and her husband are stationed in Germany with the U.S. Air Force—they do correspond regularly. "We are just so thankful to know that she saved our daughter's life!" said Leanne. "This summer, we plan to actually meet when Alyson's donor becomes stationed in the United States."

Alyson Is Still in Remission

Three years after her transplant, Alyson continues to take medication to control the rashes and upset stomach caused by graft-vs.-host disease. "Because Alyson had a mismatched, unrelated bone-marrow donor, we've learned that it can take up to six years to fight off graft-vs.-host disease," said Leanne.

Throughout her long battle, Alyson has been an inspiration to Andy and Leanne, who also have a 1-year-old son, Jack. "She has taught us so many things in life and she is living proof that you should never give up—even when the odds are against you," said Leanne. "Looking at her today, you would never know that she experienced cancer and a bone-marrow transplant. She is such a fighter."

Because Alyson experienced cancer as a baby, she never knew her life was at risk. The Looneys consider that a blessing. "She still doesn't understand any of it," said Leanne, closing the blue binder full of e-mails, "but someday she will."

A Psychologist, a Patient, and His Parents Manage Chemotherapy

Maria Sirois

Maria Sirois is a licensed clinical psychologist who works primarily with children and families facing terminal illnesses. She wrote *Every Day Counts,* from which the following selection is taken, while she was an intern at the Dana-Farber Cancer Institute in Boston. One of Sirois's patients was a five-year-old boy name Jake who suffered from acute lymphoblastic, or lymphocytic, leukemia. Jake was just beginning his treatment, but it did not take long for him to equate chemotherapy with its horrible side effects. Sirois worked with Jake and his family to help Jake understand why he needed chemotherapy and how he could count on his parents, nurses, and doctors to help him cope with his leukemia treatment.

Jake Weaver was five, a huge five, the kind of child a dad might proudly call "a bruiser." We met my first Friday on duty, three days into the training year, August 1992. A sweatpants-and-sweatshirt kid, he wore his buzz-cut brown hair under a camouflage fishing hat and carried a Teenage Mutant Ninja Turtles backpack jammed with action figures on his shoulder. In its outer zipper pouch, he stuffed a pale yellow blanket decorated with white ducklings and lambs, which, I would learn, he held during the worst exams.

Jake had ALL, acute lymphoblastic leukemia, not an uncommon cancer for a child of his age. His chemotherapy regimen required that he take pills for two weeks straight, have a week off, and begin the cycle again. He had responded well to the drugs during June and July, but now, in his tenth week, he refused to take any more pills. When faced with chemo pills at home, Jake fought hard and kept his mouth closed. In the last four days he had broken two water glasses, a breakfast bowl, one mirror, and a radio. His mom, Karen, had tried to muscle the pills into her son with no success. Her husband, Scott, had resorted to bribery and threats. Nothing worked. Jake was serious; he was done with pills.

During the four days of Jake's tirade he had taken his medicine one time out of eight. Karen had called Jake's doctor that Friday morning, demanding a meeting of Jake's team and a psychology consult. Two hours later I met Jake. . . .

Doctors Devise a Plan to Help Jake Take His Medicine

I met Jake in examining room three. Wallpapered with dancing hippos, it contained a single bed, an IV pole, a standard hospital sink and cabinetry, one swivel stool, and an infant weighing scale. Dr. Mike Sontag, Jake's physician and chief resident, introduced me to Karen and Scott. Jake was in the clinic's waiting room, playing with his favorite nurse, Jill. I stood in the doorway in order to listen to the conversation while observing Jake. As a stranger to him, I wasn't certain I was going to be able to do much good this first meeting. Mike listened to Jake's parents recount his rebellion and concurred that this was serious. Jake couldn't afford to miss meds or be in charge of his own treatment. Mike asked me what I thought we should do. New to pediatric oncology and new to children as clients, I didn't have an answer. I stalled for time by asking Mike if he had ever seen this kind of behavior before. "No," he said, "usually the kids are pretty compliant." This put the ball back in my court. Not wanting to let these parents down I suggested I page my supervisor. "She's been doing this for decades; let's see what she has to say."

I called Donna and to my surprise she was actually in her office. Briefing her over the phone at the clinic's desk I could see Jake lining up soldiers along the windowsill, explaining each one's magic powers to Jill. "This one shoots invisible laser bullets," he warned, holding a blue figure with an oversized gun in his hand. He was aiming the gun at the other children romping about in the playroom.

I moved behind the desk to keep the phone call private. I told Donna, "Mike wants this taken care of today. Jake's parents have tried the usual reward charts, threats, promises of gifts. None of it's worked. Any suggestions?"

Donna's answer was immediate and blunt. "Give him one choice, Maria. Tell him he has two minutes to take his pills right there in the office or he will be held down and forced to swallow."

"What? You want us to shove pills down his throat?" I asked. Jake had switched his attention to toy trucks, using a bulldozer to knock over enemy soldiers on the sill.

"Yes. Get everyone on the team involved except the parents. Let them be the good guys. But make sure Jake knows that they agree with the plan."

"Donna, he doesn't even know me. We have no alliance, and we don't even know why he's doing this." I watched as Jill helped Jake attack the enemy's hideout, a blue chair cushion under which Jake had hidden dinosaurs and an alien. They sneaked around to the back of the chair, Jake attacking from overhead as Jill lifted the pillow with an "ah hah!"

"Maria, you don't have time for an alliance. He has to understand now that he has no other option. As for why he's doing it, it's pretty simple. He either hates it, is afraid of it, or is too overwhelmed to care. His internal process is not as important in this moment as his chance to stay alive. You could do weeks of puppet play about this and still not know what is going on in a five-year-old's head. He doesn't have weeks."

"This is going to be hard."

"Keep it quick. Tell him once, give him the time limit, then have the team hold him down; you are not to be part of the physical restraint. You don't want his anxiety to build any more than it has to. Tell him you will do this each time he has to take meds until he does it himself at home. One more thing. It's okay that it's hard. Just think of how hard cancer is for a child."

I hung up, stunned.

Maria Attempts Persuasion

Dr. Mike and Jake's parents agreed with the plan without question. The parents had already had to make harsh choices: to keep Jake away from his friends and school to reduce the risk of infection, to change work so that someone would be home with Jake every hour each day, to drive for hours each visit to provide him with care at this hospital, instead of in their local hospital. They were relieved to have a plan.

After I took Jill aside and explained what we were going to do, she brought Jake into the examining room and invited two of the male nurses, Bill and Rich, in as well. We put Jake on the bed and I introduced myself.

"Jake, we don't know each other. My name is Maria, and I'm going to be a part of your team. Dr. Mike asked me to help make sure you take your meds. We understand from your parents that you haven't taken them lately. Is that right?"

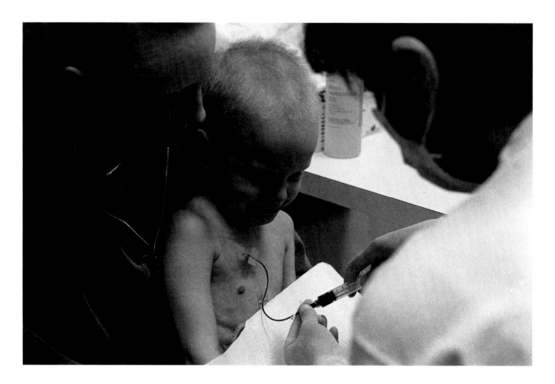

Successful leukemia treatment for children requires a joint effort by physicians, patients, and parents. (© age fotostock/ SuperStock)

Jake kept his head down and fiddled with his knees.

"So we don't really have many options because you need the medicine to make you better." I waited for a response, but Jake remained silent.

"Here's the deal then. I'm going to ask Jill to get the egg timer from the treatment room. We're going to set it for two minutes. You have those two minutes to take the pills yourself, just like you used to do at home. If you choose not to take them, then we'll have to hold you down and make you take them."

Jake glowered at me, got off the bed, and walked over to his dad. Scott said nothing, but picked his son up.

"We don't want to force you to take these pills, Jake," I continued, "but nothing is more important than getting the cancer out of you, and we need to have the medicine inside you to do that. Do you understand the deal?"

Jake pulled his dad's head down and whispered to him.

Scott shook his head. "There's no going home until you take the pills, Jake."

At that Jill got the egg timer, and Mike placed the pills on a tray on the bed. I could smell my own sweat. Scott put Jake on his lap on the bed. I put the tray on Jake's lap, and said, "Okay Jake, it's up to you. You have two minutes to take your pills." . . .

Doctors Force Jake to Take His Medicine

The timer was running. Jake turned once to his mom, who smiled through her tears and told him that she knew he could do this. He stared at the pills and for the full two minutes did nothing. No words, no fighting, no sighing, no kicking; he simply sat and let the egg timer tick away. At one minute and forty seconds, I had signaled his mom to move out of the way. Jake sat still. At one minute fifty I'd sent Mike to the head of the bed, the two male nurses to the sides, and positioned myself at the foot. I let Jill decide where she wanted to be.

When the egg timer rang, Jake jumped in his dad's lap, causing the pills to fall. I gathered them quickly saying, "Scott, please move to the door." Jake went to move with him, and I picked up this fierce, unknown boy and put him back on the bed. As I tried to lay him down, he kicked me in the neck. Mike immediately grabbed his shoulders and Bill and Rich reached to restrain his arms. Jake was struggling hard now. I went to hold his feet and remembered Donna's last-minute advice. I was not to actually be involved in the restraint. I backed off and stood instead near his knees. Jill had gone to Jake's right side and was trying to soothe him. I couldn't hear what she was saying; it took all my attention to keep myself steady.

"Jake," Mike warned, "you have to do this, buddy. We're going to be here as long as it takes. You have to do this."

The child fought, screaming and writhing, shouting for his parents to help him. His mom cried openly. Scott pressed his hands on my back, willing me to end this. I leaned forward so Jake could hear me and told him we were going to put a pill in his mouth. I signaled Mike. He held Jake's head in one arm and slipped one pill in against his cheek. Jake began to gag on the pill, and Mike lifted his head to help him swallow. Jill offered water, but Jake began shaking his head and moaning, "No, no, no, no," over and over.

"Mike, did he swallow it?" I had to shout over Jake's moans.

"I don't know. Jake, is it down?"

Jake spat the pill out at Jill, and I took it and put it back in Mike's hand. Mike opened Jake's jaw and slid the pill in, telling Jake we wouldn't give up. Jill was crying now. She pleaded with Jake to swallow. Mike's face was inches from Jake's, and he kept repeating, "It will be okay, it will be okay. You have to have the pills to make it okay." Jake's moaning quieted. He tried to sit up straight. I told him he couldn't come off the bed until all the pills were inside him. He opened his mouth to show me that the pill was gone. I signaled Mike for the next pill.

"Good job. Which one do you want next?" I was desperate to give him control over his own body. My hands trembled; I tried to hide my nervousness from him.

He looked at me mutely and I chose for him. "Jake, I'm going to give you this one next. If you want a different one, pick it now." I showed Jake a pill. He didn't move. I handed it to Mike, and he put it in Jake's mouth. This time Jake turned to Jill for water. He took the last pill soundlessly, his arms slack, his face down toward his chest. I could hear others sobbing but couldn't turn my attention away from Jake. Mucus collected in my nose and throat, tears threatening to come. There was something even more painful in his resignation than in his fighting—to break a child's spirit is a brutal act.

FAST FACT

As of 2005 there were approximately 200,000 people in the United States who were currently diagnosed with leukemia or had a history of leukemia.

Jake's Parents Comfort Him After Chemotheraphy

Bill, Rich, and I moved away from the bed to let his parents comfort him. Mike stepped back into the doorway, holding onto the lintel. Karen climbed onto the bed and gathered Jake into her arms, while Scott rubbed his back. In his mother's embrace, Jake sobbed openly. We were quiet, letting him find his way back to safety. When a few moments had passed I spoke.

"Jake, we are so proud of you, so proud." He burrowed his head into Karen.

"You're so strong," Jill cheered. "We needed four people to hold you down."

Mike chimed in, "You're the strongest kid I know, Jake." At that Jake smiled, lifting his head to look at Mike, two brown eyes cresting just above his mother's shoulder.

"Your strength is going to help you beat the bad guys," I added. "But you need extra power, just like your ninja guys, to win against the aliens. The pills are your extra power, and we aren't going to let you fight this cancer without them."

Jake didn't turn his face or meet my eyes. Who knew if my words had much impact on him, given what he had just experienced? Without a relationship, they were at best a shot in the dark. I asked Karen when he had to take his medicine again.

"After supper," she answered.

Scott picked his son up out of Karen's arms. Jake let his dad hold him for a moment, then scrambled to the ground. I knelt to speak with him face-to-face.

"Jake, Dr. Mike and the nurses are going to have to leave. I'll stay here with you and your parents and we can talk about whether you are going to take the pills at home like you used to or if you need us to help you take them again tonight." He spun away immediately and stuck his head between his father's knees.

Mike and Bill and Rich left, each giving Jake a pat on the back. Jill gave Jake a hug, repeating how proud she was of him and asking him to find her again before he left. Alone with him and his parents, I told Karen and Scott how sorry I was that we had had to do this to their son, that they were all unusually brave, and that I knew how it must have hurt them to witness his struggle. I treated Jake as if he were a much older child, writing my pager number in large print on a piece of paper and handing it to him. I explained to Jake that he needed to call me when he had made up his mind about taking the next round of medicine. Then I suggested that they might want some private time now. Ten paces down the hallway as I turned the corner I heard Scott calling my name. Jake had given them his answer. "What do you think, Jake?" I asked as I walked back to the treatment room.

"I'll take the pills by myself," he said softly.

"That's great. C'mon, let's go tell Jill and Dr. Mike." I gave him a big thumbs up. . . .

Jake Continues His Leukemia Treatment

On Monday, Jake returned for his regular checkup. He brought his superhero collection for us to play with and offered me the first pick. We were to surround the enemy (a stuffed twelve-inch-tall dinosaur) and attack simultaneously. He told me exactly where to hide my hero, when to engage, and when I'd have to take cover. Lying on the floor of the psychology intern room, I was happy and surprised. I had expected us to have to warm up to each other slowly given Friday's traumatic encounter. But Jake had his own priorities: play came first, cancer second. He understood the drill now, Karen would tell me at the end of the session. As long as Jake took his pills, his days could be full of the things he loved.

We did not have to hold Jake down again. For the length of that year, he was a compliant, loving child, who brought his toys to each session and asked only that we play together. Over time, Jake, his parents, and I became connected, and we learned as a group what Jake needed to know before each treatment or test: that he was loved, that he could play with the things he loved, and that he would not ever go through this alone.

At the end of the year, Jake brought me a handmade birdhouse, rough pieces of misaligned wood painted in the palette of childhood—sky blue, sunflower orange, neon green, lemon yellow. It was small enough for me to hold in one hand. He cradled the birdhouse against his chest, an offering of great pride. As he held it out to me, he ducked his head in a shy smile. Karen spoke for him, telling me that he and his father had crafted the house and Jake had selected the wood, the colors, and the shape. Jake had told her on the way over that he hoped I would hang it someplace where I could see it daily and be reminded of him. He wanted to say thanks for the good times we had had.

I had no words with which to respond, other than to offer a thank-you that was filled with wonder. Jake and I smiled at each other for a long moment, then gave each other a long good-bye hug.

Placing the birdhouse on my kitchen windowsill that evening I shook my head. How was it possible that this year meant good times to him? His chart was full of notes that marked a year of difficulty: vomiting; bed-wetting; anger at having to miss his friends' parties, school events, and vacation; worry that his parents would not love him if he didn't get better; mood swings; insomnia; nighttime fears. This would have been enough for me to have considered it a bad year, a very bad year.

With time, I understood something: Jake's youth and innocence supplied him with a protection and a knowledge I had forgotten. If you can live in the moment doing what you love, as children can, and you are surrounded by those you trust, then suffering is ameliorated and it becomes a part, not the whole, of your life.

GLOSSARY

acute Having a rapid onset or progression.

acute leukemia A cancer of the white blood cells with a rapid onset and progression. The two major types of acute leukemia are acute lymphoblastic leukemia (ALL) and acute myelocytic leukemia (AML).

acute lymphoblastic leukemia (ALL) A rapidly progressing form of leukemia characterized by high numbers of immature white blood cells. It is also called acute lymphocytic leukemia. ALL is the most common cancer in children.

acute myelogenous leukemia or acute myeloid leukemia (AML) A blood cancer in which too many immature cells are in the bone marrow and blood.

allogeneic Cells, tissue, and the like transferred from one individual to another.

alopecia Hair loss; a common side effect of chemotherapy.

anemia A condition in which the oxygen-carrying capacity of the blood is decreased because an individual has fewer than normal red blood cells or a less than normal quantity of blood hemoglobin.

anesthesia Loss of feeling or awareness; used in surgery and other medical procedures to control pain or keep patients unconscious.

aspiration Removal of a sample of fluid and cells through a needle.

autologous Transfer of cells, tissue, and the like from a donor to him- or herself.

benzene A colorless, highly flammable, and toxic hydrocarbon used in the production of many plastics, rubbers, and dyes.

bias	A statistical error typically caused by favoring some test groups or outcomes over others.
biopsy	The removal of a sample of tissue for purposes of diagnosis.
blasts	Immature blood cells.
bone marrow	The soft tissue inside of bones where blood is formed.
bone marrow removal	The removal of a small amount of bone marrow (usually from the hip) through a needle.
bone marrow transplant	Procedure in which bone marrow that is diseased or damaged is replaced with healthy bone marrow from a matching—that is, genetically compatible—donor. For leukemia patients, the bone marrow to be replaced is often first destroyed by chemotherapy and/or radiation therapy.
cancer	An abnormal growth of cells.
catheter	A thin, flexible tube, most often used to deliver medications or to help eliminate wastes or fluid.
cell	The basic structural unit of all living things.
chemotherapy	Drug therapy for cancer treatment; also refers specifically to the use of drugs to kill cancerous (and sometimes other) cells.
chromosomes	Carriers of the genetic material. They are composed of deoxyribonucleic acid (DNA) and proteins.
chronic	Long-lasting.
chronic leukemia	Cancer of the blood cells that progresses relatively slowly.
chronic myelogenous leukemia or chronic myelocytic leukemia (CML)	A chronic disease in which the bone marrow produces too many white blood cells. It is also known as chronic granulocytic leukemia.
clinical	Related to the treatment of patients.

clinical trials	Trials to evaluate the safety and effectiveness of drugs and other treatments by monitoring their effects over time on groups of people.
cord blood	Stem cell–containing blood from the umbilical cord.
diagnosis	The identification of an illness.
donor	The giver of a tissue or organ.
donor registry	A database of medical and personal information about potential donors. Donor registries aid in the location of matching donors for patients awaiting transplants.
Down syndrome	A common chromosome disorder due to an extra chromosome number 21 (trisomy 21), which causes mental retardation, certain facial characteristics, and multiple malformations.
genetic	Having to do with genes and genetic information.
graft	Transplanted material. In leukemia patients, a graft is typically a small amount of bone marrow received from a donor that is placed within the recipient's bones.
graft-versus-host disease (GVHD)	A complication of bone marrow transplants in which cells in the donor bone marrow graft attack the recipient's tissues. GVHD is more common when a donor is unrelated to the patient or when the donor is related to the patient but not a perfect match.
hairy cell leukemia	A rare form of chronic leukemia in which a type of malignant white blood cell called B-lymphocytes are found in the bone marrow, spleen, or blood. The disease is named for these cells, which when viewed under the microscope have hairlike projections.
hemoglobin	The oxygen-carrying protein in red blood cells.
infertile	Unable to conceive children; sterile.
interferon	A naturally occurring substance that interferes with the ability of viruses to reproduce.

leukemia	Cancer of the (white) blood cells.
malignant	Cancerous; threatening to life.
mean	A mathematical average.
outpatient	A patient who is not admitted to the hospital overnight in order to receive treatment; a patient treated in a clinic, doctor's office, or surgery center.
oxygen	A colorless, odorless, and tasteless gas necessary to life; a significant component of breathable air.
palliative care	Treatments to reduce the severity, progress, or symptoms of a disease rather than cure the disease.
pathologist	A physician or researcher who identifies diseases.
pediatric	Pertaining to children.
radiation	Rays of energy.
radiation therapy	The use of radiation from X-rays, gamma rays, neutrons, and other sources to kill cancer cells and shrink tumors. The radiation used in cancer treatments may come from a machine outside the body or radioisotopes that can be placed within the body.
red blood cells	The blood cells that carry oxygen.
relapse	The return of a disease following remission.
remission	Disappearance of the signs and symptoms of cancer or other disease; can be temporary or permanent.
risk factor	Something that increases an individual's chances of developing a certain disease.
side effects	Problems that occur during or as a result of a treatment.
spinal tap	A procedure in which fluid is removed from the spinal canal for the purposes of diagnosis or monitoring; also known as a lumbar puncture.

spleen   An organ located in the upper left part of the abdomen, near the stomach, that helps filter the blood by destroying aged, deformed, or diseased blood cells.

stem cell   A cell with the ability to grow into any one of the body's more than two hundred cell types.

stem cell transplant   A treatment for cancer or other diseases in which stem cells are removed from a donor and given to the patient.

symptom   The evidence of disease.

T-cell leukemia   A disease in which certain cells called T lymphocytes or T cells are malignant. T cells are a type of white blood cell that normally attacks foreign or infected cells.

therapy   The treatment of disease.

umbilical cord   The cord that connects a developing fetus with the placenta during gestation.

white blood cell   Several types of cells that help fight infection; also called leukocytes.

CHRONOLOGY

B.C.   **ca. 450**   Ancient Greeks are the first to recognize and describe a variety of diseases now known as cancers.

A.D.   **ca. 1240**   Arab polymath Ibn al-Nafis identifies and describes the flow of blood through the body. His discoveries remain unknown for centuries in most of the world when several Latin translations of his multivolume medical encyclopedia are lost.

ca. 1610   Italian physician Gaspae Aselli offers an early explanation of the lymphatic system.

1616   Englishman William Harvey describes the circulatory system of the blood.

1827   French physician Alfred Velpeau becomes the first modern physician to identify the disease later named leukemia. Following an autopsy, he identifies a victim's "pus filled blood" as containing an abundance of white blood cells.

1845   German pathologist Rudolph Virchow described *weisses blut* (white blood), an imbalance between white blood cells (leukocytes) and red blood cells (erythrocytes).

1845   Scottish physician John Hughes Bennett names the form of blood cancer diagnosed in one of his Edinburgh patients "leukemia."

1865   Fowler's solution (arsenic trioxide) is used as an attempted treatment for leukemia.

1890   German physician Paul Ehrlich classifies leukocytes by shape, kind, and function.

1913   Physicians agree on the classification of leukemias into four major types: chronic lymphocytic leukemia, chronic myelogenous leukemia, acute lymphocytic leukemia, and erythroleukemia.

1920s   X-ray radiation is first used to treat cancers. Shortly after its introduction, radiation is found to be both a cure for and a cause of leukemia. Many early pioneers of X-ray medicine died of leukemia.

1940s   The drug aminopterin is first used by American pediatric pathologist Sidney Farber to treat acute leukemia.

1950   American chemotherapy researchers George Hitchings and Gertrude Elion create 6-mercaptopurin, the first effective drug designed to treat leukemia. The pair developed other drugs and drug combinations to be used as early leukemia chemotherapies.

1952   Total body irradiation is used as an unsuccessful treatment for leukemia. It is later used in combination with bone marrow transplantation.

1956   E. Donnall Thomas performs the first bone marrow transplant that results in long-term survival of a leukemia patient. The donor was the patient's twin sibling.

1965   James Holland, Emil Freireich, and Emil Frei assert that cancer chemotherapy should use a combination of different drugs, each with its own therapeutic effect.

1970   Medical advances produce the first patients to achieve permanent remission and be cured of leukemia.

1973   The first bone marrow transplant from an unrelated donor takes place in New York at Memorial Sloan-Kettering Cancer Center.

1987   The National Marrow Donor Program is founded.

1988   The first successful stem cell transplant using umbilical cord blood occurs in Paris, France.

1990s   Cure rates for some leukemias reach 70 percent.

1990s   American researcher Brian J. Druker leads key clinical trials of imatinib use with chronic myelogenous leukemia (CML).

2001   Chronic leukemia-fighting drug Gleevec receives U.S. Food and Drug Administration (FDA) approval in May.

ORGANIZATIONS TO CONTACT

The editors have compiled the following list of organizations concerned with the issues debated in this book. The descriptions are derived from materials provided by the organizations. All have publications or information available for interested readers. The list was compiled on the date of publication of the present volume; the information provided here may change. Be aware that many organizations take several weeks or longer to respond to inquiries, so allow as much time as possible.

American Cancer Society
1599 Clifton Rd. NE
Atlanta, GA 30329
(800) 227-2345
fax: (866) 228-4327
Web site: www.cancer
.org

The American Cancer Society is a voluntary, nonprofit health organization that provides grants to researchers, organizes public awareness campaigns, and provides information about cancer and cancer treatment. The American Cancer Society maintains thirty-four hundred local offices within the United States. The organization provides an extensive collection of on-line resources including news of recent cancer research breakthroughs, information sheets on specific types of cancer, and articles on healthy living and cancer prevention.

Dana-Farber Cancer Institute
44 Binney St.
Boston, MA 02115
(866) 408-3324
Web site: www.dana-farber.org

Dana-Farber Cancer Institute is one of the National Cancer Institutes designated Comprehensive Cancer Centers. It is affiliated with Harvard Medical School. The institute maintains a collection of online resources and first-person narratives and also publishes the biannual magazine *Paths of Progress* and the quarterly magazine *Side by Side*, written by and for patients.

Fred Hutchinson Cancer Research Center
1100 Fairview Ave. North
PO Box 19024
Seattle, WA 98109
(800) 804-8824
fax: (206) 288-1025
Web site: www.fhcrc .org

Founded in Seattle, Washington, in 1975, the Fred Hutchinson Cancer Research Center focuses on prevention, early detection, and treatment. The center pioneered the use of bone marrow transplants to treat leukemia. Its online resources include information on clinical trials, general disease information, and updates on medical research breakthroughs.

The Friends of José Carreras International Leukemia Foundation
Muntaner, 383, 2n
08021 Barcelona, Spain
34 902 240 480
fax: 34 93 201 05 88
Web site: www .fcarreras.org/home .php?&idioma=en

Internationally renowned opera singer and leukemia survivor José Carreras founded the José Carreras International Leukemia Foundation in 1988. The foundation funds leukemia research projects and provides fellowship grants to leukemia researchers early in their careers. The organization maintains a collection of resources and public awareness campaign literature in English, with numerous additional publications, including a monthly bulletin, available in Spanish.

Leukemia and Lymphoma Society
1311 Mamaroneck Ave.
White Plains, NY 10605
(800) 959-4572
fax: (914) 949-6691
Web site: www.leuke mia-lymphoma.org/ hm_lls

The Leukemia and Lymphoma Society is the largest voluntary health organization dedicated to the research and education on leukemia and other blood diseases. Since its founding in 1949, the society has provided hundreds of millions of dollars for research on leukemia and other blood diseases. The organization provides free informational materials through its Web site in addition to its monthly *Links* newsletters.

Leukemia Research Foundation
3520 Lake Ave.
Ste. 202
Wilmette, IL 60091
(847) 424-0600
fax: (847) 424-0606
Web site: www.leuke
mia-research.org

Founded in 1946, the Leukemia Research Foundation provides grants to leukemia research projects throughout the world. The foundation also provides educational resources, emotional support, and financial assistance to leukemia patients. The foundation's Web site provides information on blood cancers, medical research, and fund-raising campaigns to benefit leukemia research.

Mayo Foundation for Medical Education and Research
200 1st St. SW
Rochester, MN 55905
(507) 284-2511
fax: (507) 284-0161
Web site: www.mayo
.edu

The nonprofit Mayo Foundation for Medical Education and Research is a research and training facility operated through the Mayo Clinic. The foundation's Web site provides general information on diseases and courses of treatment. Its searchable archives contain up-to-date information on leukemia treatment, medical and genetic research, clinical trials, and prevention.

National Cancer Institute
6116 Executive Blvd.
Rm. 3036A
Bethesda, MD 20892-8322
(800) 422-6237
Web site: www.can
cer.gov

Founded in 1937, the National Cancer Institute is part of the United States' federally funded National Institutes of Health. The National Cancer Institute is a research and development center but also provides funding to other cancer researchers in the United States. The institute maintains extensive disease-specific online resources, including the publication *What You Need to Know About Leukemia.*

National Marrow Donor Program
3001 Broadway St. NE
Ste. 100
Minneapolis, MN
55413-1753
(800) 627-7692
Web site: www.mar
row.org

The National Marrow Donor Program is a nonprofit organization that operates the federally funded registry of volunteer bone marrow donors in the United States. The program currently has almost 7 million potential donors and has facilitated over thirty thousand transplants. The organization also provides online resources about diseases, marrow transplants, marrow donation, and donor advocacy.

St. Jude Children's Research Hospital
332 N. Lauderdale
Memphis, TN 38105
(901) 495-3300
Web site: www.stjude.
org

St. Jude Children's Research Hospital is a pediatric research and treatment facility located in Memphis, Tennessee. St. Jude is the second largest health care charity in the United States. St. Jude accepts all medically eligible patients without regard to the family's ability to pay. The organization's Web site features general disease and treatment information, first-person accounts, and multimedia presentations such as *What I Want to Tell Leukemia* and the audio program *St. Jude Medical Minutes*.

FOR FURTHER READING

Books

Barbara J. Bain, *Leukemia Diagnosis.* Malden, MA: Blackwell, 2003.

Edward D. Ball, *100 Questions and Answers About Leukemia.* Sudbury, MA: Jones and Bartlett, 2007.

Federico Caligaris-Cappio and R. Dalla-Favera, eds., *Chronic Lymphocytic Leukemia.* New York: Springer, 2005.

Angelo M. Carella et al., eds., *Chronic Myeloid Leukemia.* London: Taylor and Francis, 2007.

Jorge Cortes and Michael Deininger, eds., *Chronic Myeloid Leukemia.* New York: Informa, 2007.

Judith E. Karp, *Acute Myelogenous Leukemia.* Totowa, NJ: Humana, 2007.

Lorrie Klosterman, *Leukemia.* Salt Lake City: Benchmark, 2006.

Tariq Mughal, John M. Goldman, and Sabena Mughal, *Understanding Leukemias, Lymphomas and Myelomas.* New York: Informa, 2005.

Ching-Hon Pui, ed., *Childhood Leukemias.* Cambridge: Cambridge University Press, 2006.

David A. Scheinberg and Joseph G. Jurcic, eds., *Treatment of Leukemia and Lymphoma.* Boston: Elsevier, 2004.

Joyce Brennfleck Shannon, ed., *Leukemia Sourcebook: Basic Consumer Health Information About Adult and Childhood Leukemias.* Detroit: Omnigraphics, 2003.

Periodicals

Sarah Baldauf, "After 27 Months of Chemo and Complications, It's Over," *U.S. News & World Report*, June 9, 2008.

Vickie Bane, "Marshmallow Power: Special Toy Made for Children with Cancer," *People*, July 30, 2007.

Economist, "Not So Shocking; Power Lines and Cancer," June 4, 2005.

PERSPECTIVES ON DISEASES AND DISORDERS

Ronni Gordon, "Running for My Life," *New York Times Magazine*, April 3, 2005.

Gina Kolata, "Slowly, Cancer Genes Tender Their Secrets," *New York Times*, December 27, 2005.

Daniela S. Krause and Richard A. Van Etten, "Interfering with Leukemic Stem Cells," *Nature Medicine*, May 2008.

Drew Lindsay, "Making a Match, Curing a Disease," *Washingtonian*, February 2002.

Medscape, "Unrelated Cord Blood Transplants an Option for Children with Leukemia," June 2007.

Jason Millman, "Book Gives Siblings of Ill Kids Some Much-Needed Attention," *USA Today*, April 10, 2008.

Sacramento Bee, "Going to Bat for His Sister," May 6, 2008.

Science News, "Immune Cells to Fight Leukemia," December 22, 2007.

———, "In Search of Safer Marrow Transplants," December 22, 2007.

———, "New Clue to Down Syndrome, Leukemia Link," December 22, 2007.

A. Shah, "Increasing Incidence of Childhood Leukaemia: A Controversy Re-examined," *British Journal of Cancer*, August 21, 2007.

Tulsa World, "Battling Leukemia Daily," June 4, 2008.

US Newswire, "Innovative Research Advances Stem Cell and Bone Marrow Transplantation," December 10, 2007.

Ventura County Star, "Parents Hope Sibling's Stem Cells Will Give Daughter a Second Chance: Giving Birth to Save a Life," June 1, 2008.

Women's Health Weekly, "First Step Towards Switching Off Breast Cancer and Leukaemia," August 28, 2008.

Internet Resources

American Cancer Society, "What Is Acute Myeloid Leukemia? August 3, 2007. www.cancer.org/docroot/CRI/content/CRI-2-4-1x-What_Is_Acute_Myeloid_Leukemia.asp?sitearea=.

Healthlink, Medical College of Wisconsin, "Umbilical Cord Blood Provides New Hope for Leukemia Patients," February 10, 2005. http://healthlink.mcw.edu/article/1031002472.html.

Leukemia and Lymphoma Society, "Understanding Leukemia," January 2007. www.leukemia-lymphoma.org/attachments/National/br_1172501426.pdf.

Mayo Clinic, "Hairy Cell Leukemia," www.mayoclinic.com/health/hairy-cell-leukemia/DS00673.

Medline Plus, "Childhood Leukemia." www.nlm.nih.gov/medlineplus/leukemiachildhood.html.

———, "Leukemia, Adult Acute." www.nlm.nih.gov/medline plus/leukemiaadultacute.html.

National Cancer Institute, U.S. National Institutes of Health, "What You Need to Know About Leukemia," March 2003. www.cancer.gov/cancertopics/wyntk/leukemia.

Arthur Schoenstadt, "Leukemia," EMed, October 28, 2006. http://leukemia.emedtv.com/leukemia/leukemia.html.

St. Jude Children's Research Hospital, "Molecular Science Could Further Improve Leukemia Survival, Say St. Jude Researchers," news release, March 20, 2008. www.stjude.org/stjude/v/index.jsp?vgnextoid=1c88eae31c1d8110VgnVCM1000001e0215acRCRD&vgnextchannel=708113c016118010VgnVCM1000000e2015acRCRD.

INDEX